LIFE WITH
KENNETH CONNOR

Jeremy Connor

With

Paul Burton

Published in 2014 by FeedARead.com Publishing –
Arts Council funded

A CIP catalogue record for this title is available from
the British Library.

Dedication

For Tom, Hayley and Alice with love.

And to Annie, whose constant faith and love has achieved me many goals.

'I'm like Bottom the weaver in *Midsummer's Night Dream*, one of those people who wants to do everything. If I see a barbershop quartet I want to be in it. If I see a Western, I know it's missing one thing – me. If I see a good love scene, I know I'm the man. But who's going to make room for me?'

Kenneth Connor

'When's your father going to write his memoirs?'

'Dad, when are you going to write your memoirs?'

'I can't write. You can do it if you want.'

'Jeremy, when are you going to write your dad's memoirs?'

'Jem, you really ought to write the story of your dad.'

'Dad, are you ever going to write about grandad?'

Foreword

Paul Shane and I virtually begged David Croft to cast Kenneth in *Hi-de-Hi!* He was originally asked to only make one appearance and play an old tramp, after the actor who played old Mr Partridge, Leslie Dwyer, passed away. However, Kenneth went on to play Uncle Sammy, the children's entertainer, as a permanent cast member.

The characters Ted Bovis and Spike Dixon found Sammy working as a children's entertainer on the beach. The character was later given a job at Maplin's Holiday Camp. He was really grateful for the job, and to have somewhere to live and be able to eat three meals a day. Sammy was really quite eccentric and would still take food out of the dustbins to eat!

I had been an admirer of Kenneth's all my life, but to suddenly find myself in a scene with him, where I was scrubbing his back while he was in the bath, was very funny and strange!

Kenneth had some lovely scenes with Felix Bowness, who played Fred Quilley in the series. They had nice banter. Felix also used to do the audience warm-up for *Hi-de-Hi!*, and Kenneth would sometimes goose him while he was talking!

I remember that six of us were having breakfast in the canteen at the North Acton Rehearsal Rooms (nick-named the Acton Hilton) one morning. I saw Kenneth enter, grab a tray and join the queue to get some breakfast. Because we often used to play tricks on each other during the series, I suggested to the others we play a little joke on him. They agreed. So when Kenneth joined us, we all stood up and left the table! He saw the funny side. In fact, I noticed that he was laughing so much his tray was shaking!

Kenneth was such fun to work with. He had a wicked sense of humour. I remember that we were all out one night and he suddenly started talking about beetroot and kept going on about how it turns your poo red!

I used to listen to Kenneth in Ted Ray's radio show *Ray's a Laugh* when I was a child. Kenneth used to play a character called Sidney Mincing, whose catchphrase was: 'Do you mind?' Then, in the late Eighties, I did a radio sketch show with John Inman. One week Kenneth was our special guest, so I suggested to the writers that they write a sketch where Kenneth could do his Sidney Mincing voice. And they did! It was such a wonderful thing for me to stand opposite Kenneth on stage at the BBC Paris Studio while he performed that character again.

I later worked with Charles Garland on six, five-minute TV pilots. All kinds of people were involved, including Pamela Cundell, who played Mrs Fox in *Dad's Army*. Kenneth and I appeared in one playing two sex therapists! In real life, Kenneth was very ill and frail at the time, bless him, and you could tell that he was in pain. But we did some very funny lines together. Sadly, he passed away only a few weeks later.

We missed him terribly when he died – and still do, of course. He was a national institution.

Jeffrey Holland
October 2014

Preface

I first became aware of Kenneth Connor when I started to watch the *Carry On* films and Thames TV's compilation series, *Carry On Laughing*, in the early Eighties. Although Kenneth made seventeen *Carry On* films, it is his performance as sexually frustrated Stanley Blunt in *Carry Abroad* which remains my most-favourite of all his roles in the series. Although Kenneth was a talented, serious actor, there's no doubt that he was a gifted comedy performer.

Jeremy Connor and I first came into contact in 2012. After swapping numerous messages, emails and phone calls, we finally agreed to work together on a book about his late father. It has been a sincere honour to have been able to assist Jeremy with the writing and publishing of his new publication.

Jeremy and I would both like to take this opportunity to thank a number of people for their time and help with this book. Firstly, we'd like to thank Jeffrey Holland for agreeing to write the foreword. We would also like to thank, in alphabetical order, Jonathan Cross, Shirley Eaton, Jim Eldridge, Charles Garland, Roy Gould, Anita Graham. Sherrie Hewson, Ian Lavender, Vicki Michelle, Guy Siner and Bobby Warans for contributing their recollections. Sincere thanks are also due to Jeremy's partner, Annie Connor, and his youngest daughter, Alice Connor, for sharing their memories of the late actor. We would also like to offer our gratitude to Sue Burton for her help.

I hope you will find Jeremy's memories of his life with his father, both enlightening and enjoyable.

Paul Burton
October 2014

Chapter One

Hi-Diddle-Dee-Dee

3 May 1991

The phone rang in the hall at Kenneth Connor's west London home. He could hear his wife, Micky, running to answer it. Kenny didn't move from his chair by the fire, he was tired from all the pain that goes with recovering from a major operation. He just sat and listened. All he could hear was his wife's replies:

'Who?'

'What? I beg your pardon?'

'Are you sure?"

'Really!'

'Erm... wait a minute please.'

Kenny heard the receiver being placed down on the table in the hall and Micky came into the sitting room, closing the door behind her. She looked puzzled.

'Ken,' she said, sounding rather shocked. 'There's someone on the phone saying they're from 10 Downing Street and needs to speak with Kenneth Connor in person and privately.'

Kenny sighed and slowly removed the rug that was warming his legs and made to get up.

'I bet it's that bloody Jeremy Lloyd up to one of his phone pranks!'

A cheeky smile came to his face and he went out to the hall with Micky and answered it with his gruff pirate voice.

'Who's that!?' he snapped.

A calm and confident female voice replied explaining that she was speaking from the Prime Minister's office concerning the forthcoming Birthday

11

Honours list. She mentioned that the Prime Minister would like to be reassured that the award of an MBE would be agreeable to Mr. Kenneth Connor.

'Oh, very nice indeed,' Kenny said. 'Now, who is this? Jeremy, is that you? Very funny!'

The conversation went on with a fair amount of soothing reassurance and disbelieving retorts being exchanged until the lady, who now said her name was Kitty, gave a special phone number to Kenny and asked him to ring it. That way he would have no doubts that this caller was genuine. He rang the number and it was indeed Number 10. His call was put through to Kitty, who explained that she loved this part of her job as she received so many different reactions to her announcements. Besides, she 'loved handing out surprises anyway!' Kitty said that the formal letter would be in the post that afternoon, and that they would be in contact again shortly.

Kenny and Micky had a strange remainder of the day. They suggested names of known pranksters who might be behind this, when they started doubting that it was true. They debated who they could and could not tell, and shared celebration drinks. Micky reminded Kenny that it was 'well-deserved'.

'It should have been a Knighthood!' Kenny kept joking.

However, doubt kept returning, and he started ringing around to see if he could trap a culprit. I remember he rang me at the BBC and asked me a few searching questions until he spilled the beans. I was working in David Croft`s office on *You Rang, M'Lord?*, and he knew everyone there because of appearing in *`Allo `Allo!* I congratulated him and mentioned that there were no knowing looks being exchanged in the office, so it must be true.

'It's a pain in the arse,' said Kenny. 'It means I'll have to get all my monogrammed handkerchiefs re-done.'

The following morning there was an envelope amongst the post that had 'Prime Minister' printed in the bottom left hand corner. It contained two letters, one, the official typed acceptance letter signed by Andrew Turnbull, and a smaller one that was hand written on 10 Downing Street headed paper. It read:

3/5/91

Dear Kenneth,

As promised in my telephone call to you today, herewith your letter informing you of your MBE award. (You see, I really do work for the Prime Minister!)

May I offer my sincere congratulations – this is so well-deserved. I wish you a very speedy recovery and please keep us laughing – a better tonic than any medicine – you know!

Fondest Regards,

Kitty x

6 June 1918

Kenneth Connor was born to Ellen May Connor on a Thursday in Islington, North London, just five months before the end of World War One. His father was navy officer John Francis Connor, who was known as 'Mate', and he called his wife Nell. Mate joined the Navy sometime before the start of World War One, as a midshipman, and saw conflict at The Battle of Jutland in 1916. Mate loved the navy life and was one of the RN prize boxers and long distance runners. There is still a silver trophy tankard in the family archive inscribed, 'HMS Agincourt. 1 Mile Race. Won By J. Connor. September 1916'.

The Connors soon moved down to Portsmouth, once the war had finished, so they could be near to Mate`s navy base. By the time Kenny was two years-old, Mate was chief petty officer on the Royal Yacht Victoria and Albert, and one of the leading lights of the Royal Yacht's Concert Party. One of the great joys of this position was to stage a magnificent concert for when King George V and Queen Mary were on board for Cowes Week, and various other functions. It was then, at that tender age of two, that Mate gave Kenny his first acting role as an organ grinder`s monkey. By the time he was nine, he was joined by his seven-year-old brother, Ron. The two of them performed in many charity Concert Party events. The greatest highlight for the two boys was at the Portsmouth Hippodrome, where the Royal Marine Band were dressed in the 'pip' of regalia, and Kenny and Ron sang a comedy duet. That was probably the moment when Kenny got hooked. Ronald went on to be a much respected navy doctor and G.P., while Kenny.... well, 'Hi-Diddle-Dee-Dee!'

When Mate left the navy, he took a pub on the Old Portsmouth Road called The Constitution. By doing this, he gave the sapling actor the experience necessary to play Jim Hawkins, son of the inn keeper of The Admiral Benbow pub, in *Treasure Island*.

The Constitution was a rough cider house when Mate moved his family in. There was his wife, Nell, and Kenny, Ron and little sister, Iris. Mate cleaned up the pub and painted all the cornices and pelmets with gold lacquer paint, which apparently had found its way off the Royal Yacht!

There were lots of dodgy dealings in the pub, and Mate came down hard on the clientele to straighten out the situation. Meetings used to take place where stolen goods were exchanged in the darkness of the outside toilets. Mate could handle himself, having been a boxer when in the navy, but he couldn't have eyes everywhere. So he cleverly devised an early warning alarm system. He mounted a bell at the back of the bar and tied string to the clapper. A string was led along the back of the pub, then through a series of eye hooks, up the stairs to the kids' room, and tied it off at the curtain rail. The children's window overlooked the backyard of the pub and the toilets. Mate called the kids and sat them in a row on the bed. Bringing his large round face with its boxing flattened nose up close to theirs, he spoke to them in a low, gruff, conspiratorial voice.

'I want you to keep a weather eye out for thieves and pirates,' he said. 'When you see anything suspicious, pull on this string and the bell in the bar will ring,' he continued. 'Then I'll run out and catch them red handed!'

Well, of course, this was never going to work. The fanciful minds of children looking out for thieves and pirates meant the bell was rung every five minutes. Mate ended up running out of the pub shouting and ripping open the loo doors, fists ready, the kids leaning out of the bedroom window shouting their approval. The punters soon realised what was happening.

'It's not last orders yet!' they would shout.

Mate was a natural performer and milked the situation he had created, running around with exaggerated exasperation whenever the bell rang. The punters warmed to him, and after a few months the pub took on a more family, community feel and the baddies moved away. The customers gave him the nickname Jack, a common reference for a Royal Navy sailor, and Nell started calling him that name too. They had settled in, and Kenny, being the oldest, started to help out behind the bar.

Mate had erected a flag pole in the small backyard, but it was more like a mast as it had a cross spare with stays and lines running down to anchor points in the garden walls. And there flew the Royal Ensign, probably acquired from the same source as the gold paint! Beyond the high back wall, and down an embankment, ran the steam trains into Portsmouth Harbour Station. Mate made up some boson's chairs and he would hoist Kenny, Ron and Iris up to the spar and tie them off so they could watch the trains. They just had to balance on the short plank that was the seat and hang on to the ropes. There's no doubt that they'd have Social Services on to you these days if you did anything like that!

Mate was a bit taken aback one night when an old flower lady, who was selling daffodils, came running up to the bar one day.

'Jack, you've got rats in the loos,' she cried. 'I've just had a pee and one tried to bite my arse!'

Mate looked at her sternly, and picking up a poker from the fireplace, he strode out to the ladies toilet, the old woman following close behind. The door stood open and there in the pan was a daffodil. Mate flushed the toilet and the yellow flower began revolving around the bowl.

'Tickle yer fancy?' he said grinning.

The kids, who'd heard her scream, laughed loudly as they witnessed the scene while leaning out of the window.

By 1930, Kenny was twelve and not doing too well at school. To be honest, he was just getting by. He spent too much time out on the streets with his mates getting up to no good. No drugs or glue in those days, of course, just hi-jinks and pranks.

There was a road not too far from the pub that was the main route for taking cargo away from the docks to surrounding towns. The road had a steep climb and huge horses were used to haul the carts. Halfway up there was a drinking trough for the horses to replenish themselves. One of Kenny's gang got hold of some potion that had an amazing effect on horses digestive systems, and this was added to the trough. The kids would hang around near the trough, and when the horses had been watered, the cart driver would crack the whip and whoop and encourage the horses on up the hill, the kids walking along side waiting for results. More often than not, the labouring horses would emit the noisiest and most vile farts, the driver wafting his hand while he was choking and spluttering. This had the kids in hysterics. This prank did not last long as the holder of the potion was caught in the act of pouring it in the trough, and he too was added – by a driver!

On one occasion, a fisherman's body was found floating face down just outside Portsmouth Harbour. He had fallen overboard several days earlier, and when he was pulled out of the water, the body was bloated and stiff. He had been carried to a boat shed and laid out awaiting further action. The gang decided to dare to look at the corpse that night, so after dark they gathered outside the shed daring each other to open the door and enter. When they eventually entered there was the body laid on a trestle table, it's legs up in the air due to rigor mortis. Someone, out of respect, had lit candles all around the body, which added to the macabre sight. As the kids approached a low noise started and grew in strength and pitch as the legs of the poor seaman started to lower. The foul wind still grew stronger and blow out the candles. Now the gang were screaming, running around and into each other. The stiff body of the sailor had eased in the warmth of the shed releasing the gases. The boys crashed out of the shed door running off in different directions back to their homes. The gang called this incident 'the revenge of the horses'.

Kenny's school was very small. There were few classrooms, and the hall doubled as gym and classroom. One particular day in 1932, his class were waiting in the hall for a maths lesson. Kenny was swinging on a gym rope which was suspended from a roof beam. He swung across the hall doing Tarzan impersonations, his legs out. Kenny pushed back off the classroom door for another run at it. On about the fifth swing, he was travelling back to the door when the maths teacher came in. Kenny bowled him over and knocked him out – so Kenny was out too! Yes, that's right, Kenny was expelled from school!

I must share something that I discovered while searching through the family archive for this book. I came across this interesting school report headed Portsmouth Education Committee and dated 7th March 1933:

> Kenneth Connor has been a student at the above school for nearly seven years and during that period his conduct has given every satisfaction.
>
> At all times he has worked exceptionally well and deserves great credit for the results that followed.
>
> He is a good scholar and has passed Ex St VII.
>
> He has often been given positions of trust which he filled with success.

He possesses a personality quite different to the ordinary schoolboy in as much as he fears nothing and is a fine comedian.

He is a very willing lad, reliable and trustworthy.

I recommend him, with pleasure and confidence for the position he now seeks.

G.W. Stone
Headmaster

I was confused. Kenny told me he was expelled for comedy capers, and yet this report emerges! Did he embellish the fearless comedian aspect of his report? Or was the report a forgery to apply for a job or maybe a scholarship?

Kenny started working full time in the pub and took drama lessons, which he excelled at. Later, he recalled how he set about starting his career in the acting profession during an interview with Roy Plomley on Desert Island Discs:

'Well, it was again my father. He went to see Jessie Matthews at the King's Theatre, Southsea, and took me in with him, forced his way in he did. I was most embarrassed. And she said, elocution lessons first and foremost, and that's what I did. I went on and played Shakespeare in an amateur way in Portsmouth, and then came to the Central School of Drama in London.'

Kenny's drama teacher put him up for a scholarship at Central School of Drama in London – and he was successful. So he was packed off to London and moved in with relatives in Islington. Central, which is now in Swiss Cottage, was based at the Royal Albert Hall in those days. It was founded in 1906 by Elsie Fogerty, a drama teacher who had been trained at the Paris Conservatoire. The school occupied the upper level of the Royal Albert Hall and this became his base to study his chosen art.

Kenny often spoke of another actor who sometimes trained at Central and joined the Bristol Old Vic with him after the war – his name was Patrick Troughton. Patrick was a great character actor and became the second Doctor Who for three years. Troughton was a motorbike fanatic. So much so that he would bring his bike up to the top floor of Central to prevent it from being stolen. Lunch break was Troughton's dare devil time. He would speed round the Royal Albert Hall and give anyone willing rides on the back of his bike.

When Kenny finished at Central in 1936, he left with the Gold Medal. It wasn't long afterwards that he was cast in his first professional acting role. The production was J.M Barrie's new biblical play, *The Boy David*.

Other theatre work followed, including Shakespeare at the Open Air Regents Park. And in 1939, Kenny made his first film – *Poison Pen* – in which he played the role of 'Boy in Post Office'. This was followed by the outbreak of the Second World War.

Kenny admitted on *Desert Island Discs* just how financially difficult his early years in the profession were:

'Do you know, one night in the war I was on guard, and, to keep myself awake, I worked out how much I had earned as a professional actor in those three or four years. And I still cannot get it above ten shillings a week average!'

Thankfully there were better days set to come.

Chapter Two

The War Hero

Kenny blamed his lack of culinary taste and skill on his enforced years in the army as a war hero. What? You didn't know he was a war hero?! Well, I say hero – he was, and remains one, in my eyes at least, because he survived. And I don't think he ever fired a shot in anger. He never said he killed anyone but I know his life was often in danger. The reason I am convinced he didn't kill anyone is because of his reaction to something that was disclosed to him by another actor, many years later.

When Kenny was working on the BBC sitcom, *Hi-de-Hi!*, he became friends with the diminutive actor and renowned warm-up artist, Felix Bowness (catchphrase, 'Some people think I'm gay... I'm not even sodding happy!'). One day they started talking about their experiences of World War Two. Felix told Kenny that he'd been decorated for bravery and my father managed to get him to reveal why.

Felix had been with a platoon of soldiers who were pinned down by the Germans, somewhere in France. He said there was no way out. No solution. He was very scared, and so scared that he had to do something, because no-one else was. So he grabbed a machine gun off its mounting. These are very heavy, and he was so slight. His fear must have created this newly-found, super human strength. All was quiet. There had been no gun fire for some time. Felix then jumped out of his fox hole and ran towards the direction of where he thought the Germans were, firing as he went. His instincts were correct. He mowed the lot down and then collapsed into a heap. Felix had saved all his comrades, but it sent him quite mad for a while, apparently. Having worked with him, I'd argue that he never fully recovered from the experience. When Kenny told me of this experience, it was with a sort of an incomprehension, not disbelief. As he told Felix's story you could see he was trying to put himself in that position and he could not.

'How could you kill all those people and live with it?' he said. 'Be able to function?'

Kenny's inability to be able to relate to this was proof enough for me that he had never shot anyone. He had often been in danger, though. He once even had a gun thrust into his guts by a very nervous British officer.

Kenny was, for a while, a motorbike messenger. He was not a natural biker, in fact he was crap – and would admit it!

'Why would you use two wheels when four will do?' he would say with a glint in his eye.

One night, Kenny was told to take a message from his camp to another as it was urgent. He was also told to stay there and return by daylight. Kenny had been given a map, but everywhere was in a state of blackout, of course. And with only a slit of light allowed out of the bike's headlight, and the seldom aid of a scudding moon, he became hopelessly lost.

Eventually, Kenny came across a camp and approached with caution. There were two guards talking to an officer at the barrier and they immediately raised their guns as they heard the bike approach. He stopped and announced himself in the correct manner giving name, rank and number and purpose.

'Hands up!' the officer replied. 'Do not move, or you will be shot!'

He then approached my father. Kenny was still straddling the noisy bike, his arms held high. The officer thrust his pistol deep into his stomach, turned the thumping engine off, and demanded he repeat his name, rank and number. Kenny could feel the shaking hand of the officer through the barrel of the pistol as it pressed further into his guts.

'Steady, Sir. Friend not foe,' he managed to reply. 'I think I may be lost.'

'Name, rank and number!' screamed the officer.

Kenny replied. By now, he was shaking and could feel his guts turning to water.

'Stay still,' said the officer, and shouted to the guards. 'Get a torch over here and shine it in his face.'

Both the guards approached, one pointing his gun straight at Kenny`s head, while the other lowered his to bring out his torch. He shone it full into his face, bringing him into full light. The officer jabbed his gun into Kenny`s ribs and then removed it.

'Fucking hell, Connor!' he bellowed. 'What the hell are you doing back here?! You were supposed to stay at the other camp overnight, you idiot!! I could have shot you. You're fucking useless!!'

It turned out that Kenny had done a random circle and ended up back at his own base, the message undelivered. The guards and officer were of course not expecting a bike to turn up. So when the rider announced himself as Private Connor, they smelt a rat. Private Connor was meant to be elsewhere. This was an imposter. The reason lay in the message he was carrying. It was a high priority message to be on high alert for parachuting German soldiers posing as British troops. And all this took place in the sleepy countryside of Sussex, while England awaited the invasion of the German might.

Kenny hated army life. It was imposed on him, as it was for millions of others, but particularly as he had just started making his way in theatre when he was called up. He was aiming to be a serious actor, playing the leads and was getting there. This was no mean task for a 5ft 5" actor at a time when you had to have height and stature to be cast in such roles. Kenny had also found himself cast in one edition of the popular *Bandwagon* radio series. Is it any wonder he felt so frustrated? With this in mind, Kenny wrote in desperation to a BBC producer in June 1939. In the letter he said:

'You know, it would not surprise me if the government have forgotten such a profession as ours exists. How they can guarantee my job back is a source of wonder to me.'

The government had promised that after call up for six months training you would return to your job. But six months turned into six-and-a-half years and the war definitely changed the course in which his acting was developing, for ever. He felt he was robbed of nearly seven years of his career. To make up for this disappointment, he used the army to keep himself physically fit and treated them as a sort of a travel agent. But getting into concert parties eluded him for some time, and his final effort to do so placed him in a court-marshal position, stripping him of his unwanted sergeant stripes. This hatred seems a little out of sorts when you realise that his father had a great time in the Royal Navy and his brother becoming a navy doctor in the war.

After call up you went to your regiment to be kitted out. Kenny was seconded to the Middlesex Regiment as a signaller, and the uniform was the first pet hate. He had sensitive skin and the cheap, rough material gave him constant rashes which he had to learn to live with. However, this 'life experience' came in handy many years later. This was when Kenny had to sweat his way through a show in a woollen costume each night as part of a demanding two-year run.

The army was a slow start of marching and cleaning, and once a week you went into a long queue to get your pay. It was two shillings a day to fight for your country.

'Hardly seems worth turning up for the wait,' he once remarked.

One morning, when Kenny was waiting in the queue, a red Mercedes open top sports car turned up, screeching to a halt. It was piled high with golf clubs and out stepped a 'poorly' soldier and walked straight down the line of waiting payees and disappeared into the office. He instantly appeared again with a pay packet, which he stuffed into his breast pocket as he rushed back to his car.

'Sorry chaps,' he said. 'I'm late for tee off.'

With that, he jumped into his car and sped off into the distance. Kenny's eyes fixed on him and recognised him as none other than the actor Peter Ustinov.

'There's got to be a way to do that,' he muttered under his breath.

On 10 May 1940, the Germans struck westward across Europe. Within just three weeks Holland and Belgium had surrendered and the Panzer Divisions had split the French and British troops. Some of the troops were trapped near the port of Dunkirk.

On 26 May, neighbouring Calais was captured and that evening back in England the Admiralty announced 'Operation Dynamo'. This was the plan to evacuate the four hundred thousand troops from Dunkirk. This seemingly impossible task was given to Vice Admiral Bertram Ramsay and his small team to accomplish. He was given less than a week to prepare; and there, at his HQ under Dover Castle, he plotted to save Kenny!

I don't know when Kenny arrived at Dunkirk or how long he stayed on the beach. All I know is how he and his platoon escaped. They had been watching the ships and boats approaching. They had seen the soldiers standing up to their chests in water holding their rifles above their heads. They had taken cover under trucks when the enemy fighter planes had strafed the beach. They had a captain who was younger than any of them. He did not fancy standing up to his neck in water. Bless him, he could not swim and he was very scared, so the others decided to take command.

Someone had spotted a sort of punt that was lying on a tank transporter and it had oars. They went up the beach to retrieve it and brought it back, guarding it for their own use. Their plan was to wait until a destroyer 'got nearish'. Then they would all dash into the water with the boat, and row out quick past the wading soldiers and be first to the ship. So they sat and waited for the moment.

It was a long wait before a smallish war ship came reasonably close and the young captain, his confidence boosted by the fact that he wasn't going to have to swim for it, made the call. They upped the boat, ran down the beach and into the water. Running and pushing the boat out, they started jumping into it. The adrenalin was rushing and they were shouting and laughing. Oars were made ready and then they realised there were no rowlocks. There was nothing to hold the oars in place. They could not row! The boat fell silent. Suddenly, Kenny noticed that that the vessel was taking on water. Shit! As the soldiers were climbing on, the more weight there was in the vessel. This meant that more the water came in through the bullet holes in the hull. The punt had been hit when the fighters strafed the beach. Thankfully, Kenny`s sea knowledge, gained from his practical and methodical father, suddenly clicked in.

'Right lads. Helmets off. Start bailing,' said Kenny. 'Two volunteers to be rowlocks'.

'I'm not being a bollock for no one,' said one sapper. Kenny managed to laugh before continuing.

'Right, rowlock boys, make a crook of your elbow and put your arm over the side of the gunwale,' he demonstrated. 'Quick. Now put the oars through the crook. Row boys, row!'

The young captain had flipped at the sight of the water coming in. And as they rowed and bailed, he stood up, jumped overboard and just sank. No one saw him again. They could not stop as they were sinking, and the incoming water was beating the bailing. They rowed and bailed for their lives. The destroyer loomed closer as they rowed past the wading soldiers who were shouting 'Jammy bastards' and 'Send it back for us'.

When at last they reached the ship, they saw a scramble net and ropes at the ready hanging down the tall side of the grey hull. Kenny ordered all to keep bailing until it was their turn to get off. One by one they left and scrambled up the net leaving Kenny until last. He then donned his helmet, which still had water in it, and grabbed a rope. Kenny looked back down at the punt just to see it disappear beneath the waves.

It was a short three hours journey back to England. They lay on the decks exhausted and smoking. Mugs of tea and spoons of jam, a mint jelly to stop sea-sickness, were being handed out for the third time when they hit a mine outside Dover Harbour. The ship came in to dock with the bows getting lower in the water. All were safe, and the ship rested itself in the shallows of the wharf. The troops disembarked and met trains to take them back to their loved ones who lived in bombed cities around the country.

Just prior to Dunkirk, Kenny had been based on the French/Belgium border, still with his messenger bike. One day he was ordered to be part of an armed escort for a staff car to take some high ranking officers to another area. He was to be the following escort. Off it set at high speed, which Kenny wasn't prepared for, and he just could not keep up the pace and soon the convoy faded into the distance. He wasn't going to kill himself with reckless driving.

Just as Kenny was ambling his way back to base, wondering how he was going to talk his way out of this situation, a stray missile went off nearby and the force of the explosion blew him off the bike. He picked himself up and was surprised to find he was quite unharmed. But looking down at the bike he realised a piece of shrapnel had gone right through the engine rendering it useless. Craftily, he quickly realised that this was more than a good enough excuse for not keeping up.

Kenny was just counting his blessings when a little old lady came out of a cottage with a cup of tea and a tool; a little red wooden hammer. It was the sort of early learning toy hammer used for banging pegs into holes. He thanked her for the tea, but declined the hammer. Kenny kissed her hand and set off on foot feeling much safer.

A few weeks passed and Kenny was sent back to the same village to lay wires for field telephones. There was a party of soldiers doing this working separately. The village was now a ghost town, the residents having fled before the advancing Germans arrived. The wires had to be concealed by covering them with earth, running them up walls covered with ivy, pinning them under eaves of the cottages etc. It was not an enviable task.

Kenny entered one house and went upstairs to look at the possibility of using the gutters to run the cable along. Everywhere was deathly still, and he went into a bedroom where it was evident there had been a quick departure. The wardrobe doors were hanging open and draws were unclosed, so he could imagine the hasty packing and the fear. He noticed a shiny top hat in the wardrobe, and pushing his tin helmet back off his head, so it hung down his back on its strap, he tried on the top hat and looked at himself in a mirror. As he was miming a toff, curling an imaginary moustache, he became aware of a moaning sound. Kenny went to the window to see where the noise was coming from. He looked down and noticed a small barn. The moaning appeared to be coming from there.

Kenny went down and out to the barn and pulled open one of the doors. Inside there was a cow tethered to a post and moaning with pain, her udder full to bursting point. He looked around and finding a milking pale he drew up a box and sitting on it he started milking the cow. With almost instant relief, it stopped moaning. He decided to start singing a song to help calm the cow.

Meanwhile, an officer checking to see how the cable laying was going in the village heard the sound of Kenny singing. Wondering what was going on, the said officer eventually discovered Private Connor wearing a top hat, milking a cow and singing 'Alouette, gentille alouette'!

Kenny was angry until his death about the seven-year detention on his path to acting success until the stop sign went up and he was on full revs! He did not like the word 'NO' and hated discipline that was non-productive. He would rebel and fight. So, using his acting skills of observation, he watched how the army system worked. Then found the right people to manipulate to enable him to get the word out that Kenneth Connor was still here, despite the war, and was ready and willing to fight. Not to fight for the army, though, but to fight for the right to entertain the British people. He had approached his commanding officer about forming a concert party for morale purposes.

'This is not a time for the frivolous pass times you wish to pursue,' he barked. 'There's a war on you know!'

Kenny had so far been a model soldier. Well, he must have been because now he was an acting sergeant, but not for long. Through the army acting grapevine, he heard about a concert party called *Stars in Battledress*. This company was full of established actors including William Devlin, who would become a good friend. In fact, it was Devlin who helped reignite Kenny's acting career after the war.

Another of the key members of the company was an actor called Geoffrey Keen (who played 'M' in six of the James Bond films) who was somewhat established as an actor already and had rank in the Royal Army Medical Corps. Kenny made contact with him and it was suggested that he should write to Keen's commander-in-chief to request for a transfer to the regiment of the 15th Scottish, as he was required for entertainment services there. Well, talk about the shit hitting the fan!

It wasn't long before the commander of the Middlesex Regiment received Private Connor's transfer request. He then angrily summoned Connor to his office.

'What's the meaning of this, Connor?' he asked. 'How dare you go above my head and seek a regiment transfer without going through ME first.'

By now the commander's cheeks were red with anger.

'You have stepped outside your regiment and by doing so I am stripping you of your stripes and you will leave this regiment forever. If you are not out of this camp by eleven hundred hours you will be court martialled. Now, get out of my office!'

Kenny said nothing. He saluted, did an about turn and left, closing the door silently with a click, just for the annoyance factor, and ran back to his billet. After handing in his stripes, and various other adornments belonging to the regiment, Kenny, already packed, left for the 15th Scottish without any regrets.

I'm not sure of the exact year this transition took place, but it was before 1942, the year he met Micky, later to be his wife, in Northumberland. But it was definitely after his time in France and his escape and rescue from Dunkirk.

Joining the 15th Scottish meant a move north, not to Scotland, but to northern England and Northumberland in particular. Kenny was now well-established with the concert party and knocking out the shows with no sign of going into action again. They had found some rehearsal rooms at a hotel in the rural town of Morpeth, north of Newcastle. They were using the ballroom of the Queens Head Hotel, a lovely building with a Tudor frontage in the centre of the town.

One day at rehearsals, Kenny was suffering with his nervous stomach and had cramp pains, so he went to reception to see if they had any pain killers. And that is where he met Micky who was the receptionist. It was love at first sight. And so, like it or not, she had to learn to live with his nagging stomach for the next fifty years!

Micky was from a farming and mining background. Kenny fell for this pretty, little Geordie girl, who used to sneak out of her bedroom window, along with her sisters in their dancing dresses, their sling backs clutched in their hands, and run down the lane to the village hall or to town and meet up with Kenny and the other soldiers.

Kenny and Micky were married within six months at a church in Morpeth with the division providing a Guard of Honour. I'm not sure if they had much of a honeymoon. They might have been given a night in the best room at the Queens Head as a wedding present from the management. Certainly no-one had any money to speak of, and both of them were from relatively poor backgrounds.

The couple had fun in those uncertain times in the rural north away from the big danger areas, but it was not long, with the war escalating, that the regiment was ordered to move south to London. Kenny did not know what to do about his new bride, but Micky made the final decision – she was going south no matter what. Unwilling to argue, Kenny decided to arrange accommodation for his new spouse with some of his relatives in Islington in north east London.

It was a real culture shock for the country girl to come to terms with the big smoke and the London accent. But she got on famously with her new relatives, and when her husband was soon posted overseas, she stayed in London waiting for him to return. No, Micky did not go back to the relative safety of Morpeth and her sisters. If he was going to be in the thick of it, then so was she. Micky was called up to work in a munitions factory, and that's where she learnt to swear.

When Micky was at home in London she would lean out of the bathroom window smoking and listening to the doodle-bug bombs flying overhead. These jet propelled flying bombs made a crackling noise as the propellant burned and when the fuel ran out, that was when they fell. Micky and her new family would count the seconds from engine cut out to explosion. To pass the time, they used to bet on how many seconds it would be!

I don't know much else about Micky's war other than on VE Day she went down to Piccadilly Circus to celebrate. After kicking off her shoes, she was hauled up on to the roof of a bus shelter and danced the night away. She never did find the shoes and walked home bare foot while breathing in the fresh air of freedom.

Meanwhile, Kenny had become quite the tourist. He was in Italy for quite a while and learnt the language to a passable level, hanging out with the locals in Naples, he discovered his passion for pasta. He wasn't one for experimenting with food, erring on the side of caution, and was therefore amazed that there was a pasta dish with bacon and eggs! The Italians used to knock it out for the troops. It was a sort of partisan Carbonara. Diced bacon fried with onions and then folded through the spaghetti, a raw egg cracked over the top, the heat of the steaming pasta cooking the egg.

One time, Kenny was sitting outside a Naples café and had ordered sardines and potatoes. When the plate arrived, there was one sardine laying on a bed of lettuce and a couple of boiled spuds on the side. The waiter looked furtively at the other diners tables and then at Kenny. He then gesticulated with his hands some information. Holding one hand out flat and horizontal, he brought up his other hand under the first and made the movement of a swimming fish, then winking at

Kenny he quickly walked away. After a few minutes of confusion, the penny dropped as he got the mime. Lifting up the salad leaves cautiously, he revealed three more sardines. Great! And so as not to get the waiter in trouble, he brought out the sardines one by one, each time hiding the bones of the precious delicacy under the leaves.

Kenny saw all the sites. He went to Pompeii and climbed Vesuvius dangling his legs over the crater and feeling the hot air on his legs. He then went through Greece and spent time in Palestine and then in Malta, where he got an old fisherman to sail him around the nearby island of Gozo.

But Kenny's travels weren't over yet. He ended up in Egypt and a stinking Cairo where they were billeted in a squalid building. The caretaker of the building would squat over a paraffin primus stove cooking fried eggs in dirty oil and charge the solders for them. So it was hardly surprising that they all contracted terrible gastric bugs.

It was here that while recovering from yet another bad stomach, and awaiting demob, that Kenny received a telegram from the actor William Devlin inviting him to join the newly forming Bristol Old Vic on his return. Suddenly his worries at the outset of war about never being able to act again were immediately lifted and fizzled away into thin air. All he had to do was wait and get home alive, the only enemy now being the terrible catering.

Just before I close this chapter on Kenny's war years, I want to share with you the contents of a postcard I found in the family home after Kenny and Micky had both passed away. It was an average, plain postcard, which I discovered in an envelope that was addressed to:

Petty Officer John. F. Connor
P.O. Mess No 30
H.M.S. Vernon
Portsmouth
Hants.

Written in pencil was the following message:

Aldershot

Sunday 2nd June

My Pop,

Whose presence was always with me, whose calmness I have inherited & have had made manifest to me, I am safe home after the Belgium Battle.

I have had a tough time finishing up in a leaking punt to catch a minesweeper before she moved off.

I made it and as they through me a rope I exclaimed:

'Capt. Silver reporting aboard, Sir!'

See you soon, dad,

Love,
Ken

Chapter Three

Kenneth In Civvy Street

After being demobbed, Kenny found himself beginning an artistically rewarding stint of eighteen months at the Bristol Old Vic, performing a variety of roles in classic and modern plays. These included *Macbeth*, *The Seagull*, *Twelfth Night*, *The Importance of Being Earnest*, *An Inspector Calls* and *Playboy of the Western World*.

Following his time in Bristol, Kenny then spent nine months at the Old Vic in London. There he played roles in productions including *The Government Inspector*, *The Taming of the Shrew* and *The Merchant of Venice*.

Kenny later related what happened during the period immediately after his spell at the Old Vic in London when he was a guest on *Desert Island Discs*:

'The bottom seemed to fall out of things for a moment or two. I did some concert part work in Brighton. That was rather like going back to what I did in the army, so I didn't like that very much. And then I came to London where I played a lovely part in *Queen Elizabeth Slept Here* at the Strand Theatre.'

Written by Talbot Rothwell, who would in time write roles for Kenny in the *Carry On* films, *Queen Elizabeth Slept Here* included Jimmy Hanley and acting royalty, and husband and wife team, Michael Denison and Dulcie Gray, in the cast. The play ran for approximately a year. After which he left the theatre for around eight years in order to concentrate on taking part in radio shows. Kenny took over from Peter Sellers in

Ted Ray's radio show, *Ray's a Laugh*. This is where the character of shopkeeper Sidney 'Do you mind' Mincing was born.

In total, Kenny was with Ted for at least eight years, before going on to play his brother-in-law on TV. I knew an old BBC technician who worked on Ted Ray's TV shows. They went out live so all the fast scene changes had to be executed in total silence. For instance, one week there was a dining table which was laid for breakfast at the start of the episode. The table was then quickly flipped over while a scene was taking place on another set to reveal it was already set for dinner. The secret to making this quick change possible was that everything was glued down!

Kenny also took part in Eric Barker's radio show *Just Fancy*. He shared his memories of working with Eric on *Desert Island Discs*:

'I often feel that acting in these little vignettes of Eric Barker will always stand me in good stead for microscopic observation parts in films and plays in the future. They were wonderful things to play.'

But as well as the comedy roles on radio, even standing in for a sick Peter Sellers on *The Goon Show*, Kenny was also cast in a number of serious roles in radio plays broadcast on the Third Programme.

Kenny was on stage in the West End the night I was born on 5 October 1955. Or, as Micky liked to say, '5th of the 10th 55 in Ward 10 at 10 past 10 on a stormy night'. The birth was not easy, thirty-six hours, and although it was not the trend for expectant fathers to attend the birth in those days, I think he would have been pacing the waiting room if all had gone to plan, but the show must go on!

Margaret Irene Churchill Knox (for that was Micky's real name) had been married to Kenny for thirteen years before that stormy night and I had been diagnosed as flatulence until she was seven months pregnant. Stop sniggering! Anyway, there were two Connors giving birth that night in Barnet General Hospital, and one of them sadly died in birth.

Kenny rang the hospital from the stage door to see how things were going and was told that he had a healthy baby but his wife had not made it. He dashed to the hospital and rushed into the reception to see Micky flat out on a bed, eyes shut and flowers laid on her chest and being wheeled out by nurses. Imagine the shock. And imagine the double shock when his wife's eyes opened.

'Hello, the baby's in the delivery room,' she said. 'I'm not doing this again!'

The other poor Connor lady had died. Micky had been in hospital for the previous week with high blood pressure, and the flowers had been sent from well-wishers. So that was Kenny's stressful entrance into fatherhood and why I'm an only child, because Micky stood by her words!

My first memory of my life with Kenny came about on yet another stormy night at our home in Barnet, north London. I had woken up crying, scared of the thunder, so he took me into the kitchen and gave me some melon. It was a huge slice and he had given me a huge spoon to scoop the flesh off with. A huge thunder clap came and I bit down on the spoon and it got wedged between my front teeth. Kenny sang a song while he clamped my head in his arm and pried the spoon out. I was about two.

We moved to Harrow when I was just old enough to remember. Now, Kenny had lived in Harrow before, and my grandad – Mate – had lived there for a while. And when Kenny saw a house for sale in a nearby country lane, an unmade road, all pebbles and flint and stone, he fell in love with it. He took Micky to see it but it was a bit of a wreck.

Built in 1928 by an architect, who had built others in the same style in the area, this particular house had been built for himself. It was called Home Oaks for obvious reasons, and is now called The Squirrels, because they eat acorns. You should never rename a ship!

The house in South Hill Avenue, Harrow-on-the-Hill, had oak floors and beams and oak panelled walls. It had an old furnace in the breakfast room and a nearby coal room accessed via the kitchen door. It was, without doubt, a mini mansion that had a butler's pantry with a servery to the oak clad dining room. There was a master bedroom, with hallway entrance, which was en-suite, despite being built back in 1928! Built on a third of an acre, Kenny bought it for £5,500.

During the war, Home Oaks was requisitioned by the Royal Navy for administration purposes. To this day, you can still see blue/black circles on the oak window sills made by the ink wells they used. When the navy moved out, it housed seven polish refugee families, and when Kenny found it, it was empty. We moved in just as the huge building works were getting underway. The house had no damp course, so trenches were dug out all round and I, as a two-year-old, was warned not to go near. Yeah, right! So when I turned up at the outside kitchen door with our two white Maltese terriers all covered in clay and soaking wet, Micky, understandably, went ballistic.

'By ya could 'ave droned ya silly bairn,' she screeched!

39

We all got washed down and sat by the furnace to warm. Kenny wasn`t there to witness the scene as he was working.

Not long after we moved into Home Oaks, Kenny and his brother, Ron, a doctor, decided to help Mate out by purchasing a house for him. Mate had suffered a bad run on jobs and was retired with only a small naval pension. A cottage had come up for sale opposite Home Oaks. It was a white painted cottage and the oldest house in the avenue, having started its life as a pottery in the late 1800`s, which is about the same time as John Francis was born.

Kenny used to play all his comedy records to me. These included the memorable song 'Two Little Men In A Flying Saucer'. He would get out his collection of military bands and play the marches at full blast while we marched up and down acting the clown. This became a Sunday morning routine, especially when I had my little friends over. He would firstly line us all up and then we`d all march off round the house. We'd go over all the beds and furniture with Micky telling Kenny off – but joining in all the same!

There were always cock-ups and misdemeanours that fortunately ended in laughs. Here`s one, just to set the style of our close relationship. Kenny loved the garden at Home Oaks. There were massive rose beds that he tended for his wife, who loved them so much. But he could not manage to produce a decent bonfire. Micky used to give him such grief about it. He`d build a small fire and start it, but then smother it with more garden cuttings. Suffocating the establishing flames.

One autumn Saturday, I was helping in the garden while Micky was cooking a best end of neck for lunch. We had stacked the bonfire ready to light. Matches were struck and newspaper lit, but the wet leaves defeated all of our efforts to consume all that were placed on the pyre.

'Jeremy, where's your water pistol?' asked Kenny in desperation.

We went into the garage with the pistol and he filled it with petrol from the lawn mower supply and off we went to the fire. I was very impressed about what was going to happen. We approached the dying fire and Kenny pulled out the fuel, loaded the gun and squirted the fire. The fire burst into flames and with amazement we watched the flames travel up the squirt to the pistol. By now, Kenny was getting the signal that all may not turn out for the good and threw the toy away. Bang and whoosh it went, a fire ball in mid-air! The plastic melted and solidified on the lawn and the bonfire died out as the rain began to fall.

'Mmm, I'll buy you another one,' he assured me. 'Don't tell your mother!'

Then there was the time that Kenny built a rockery at the top of the back garden. This area had been the site of a large clump of horseradish. That was until he dug it up and destroyed it in a fit of anger. The reason being was that he had bought Micky the latest Sunbeam cake mixer, which came with loads of intriguing attachments, including a shredder/grater – very innovative in those days! He decided to make his own horseradish sauce. Now the root of the horseradish is very tough, and the new machine not so! When he introduced a large root to the spinning grater it was bounced around violently and then jammed up the mechanism. Kenny was not to give up and turned up the speed dial. Bang it went and with a little bit of blue electrical smoke too!

Now not in the best of mood, Kenny unplugged the machine and carried out to the dustbin and hurled it in.

Micky threw the other attachments after him and they went in the bin as well. Neither of them spoke during the incident, and Kenny went to the tool shed and took a spade to the horseradish patch while Micky took out her old mixing bowl and whisk!

Prior to being destroyed by Kenny, the rockery was successful for a year or two, with lobelia and alyssum and suchlike being planted amongst the rocks. One spring day, Kenny noticed that there was a hole in the earth. A tunnel leading under one of the rocks. Some rats had settled there. What to do? Out came the garden hose, which was then thrust down the rat hole, and left running for a few hours. It flushed them out never to return. The invaders of the rockery were routed. But just like England, there have been many invaders.

Come the end of August, a wasp nest had established itself in the hollow that remained of the rat nest. What to do? Kenny imagined G.I.s recapturing a hill from the Japs. Flame throwers fired into gun emplacements to flush out the screaming enemy. Out came the lawn mower petrol can and an old rag. Thinking it would solve the problem, Kenny poured the entire contents of the can into the hole saving enough to soak the rag, which he twisted and pushed gently into the opening of the settlement. He lit the fuse and retreated rapidly. The rag was ablaze, and then it happened. WOOOMPPH!! The entire rockery swelled and lifted in to the air, earth and rocks flying everywhere. The debris of rocks was later used as a base for a new fish pond some twenty yards to the left of the destroyed rockery. Tall dahlias were planted over the war zone.

There was a problem while digging out the four foot deep kidney-shaped pond. A sewer pipe was uncovered and when completely exposed it was encased in concrete with a swim through tunnel for the fish. This became home to much prized Koi Carp, Shubunkins, Tench, water snails and regular gold fish. A Japanese style white wooden bridge spanned the pond, where tall bull rushes grew.

Kenny's hobby of gardening also stretched to building a camp in the garden for us both. The camp was built out of branches in the shrubbery in the front garden and heavily camouflaged. All the kids at Orley Farm School used to build them in the fields at summertime. It was sort of a school tradition.

One particular summer, Kenny attended the annual demonstration organised by the RAF. They flew in using a Westland Whirlwind and did displays in the cricket field. They often caused damage to the field by sinking into the cricket square, and one year, while showing off the craft's agility at low level, they took out one of the park benches turning it into matchwood. After the field show there was a talk and film in the assembly hall. Kenny walked back from the fields with one of the pilots. Passing the hedges, he asked what the pilot thought of the camps. The pilot was amazed and frustrated at the same time.

'I've just spent a tour in Vietnam in the jungle,' he replied. 'And I didn't even notice one until you pointed them out.'

Kenny soon spread this news around the school and to all the parents. This is what inspired him to build in our garden. Always the kid!!!

I definitely inherited some of Kenny's traits. One time, a school friend told me that fireworks still work under water if you let the fuse start actually sparking before putting in water. When I was about fourteen, another friend and I decided to try it out with a banger. To make it work you had to wrap the base of the banger in wet clay, so it would sink. We went up to Kenny's much prized fish pond and were preparing for the experiment, when this image came into my head of a news item I had seen on the BBC. The report covered the modern day poacher of trout, where instead of tickling the trout and flipping it out of the water, which was a great skill handed down through generations, you just threw a hand grenade into the lake and on detonation all these stunned and dead trout bobbed up to the surface.

'No, No! Not the fish pond. If that kills the fish, I'm dead too!' I pleaded. 'Let's try it out in the rain butt'.

Now, the rain butt was on the side of the house in an alleyway leading to the garage courtyard. It was an old wine barrel mounted on bricks with a down pipe from the gutter going into the top and a brass tap at the bottom to draw off the water. This was only a short distance from the site of the exploding rockery. We lit the banger and the fuse started to fizz and we dropped it into the butt and down it sank. Silence. Jimmy Morris had lied. I had been conned and now embarrassed in front of my friend Ian. Then BANG and a tower of water shot out of the barrel, the hoops twanged apart and the wooden slats parted company, then a torrent of water tsunamied down the alley gathering immense speed.

Micky was hanging out laundry in the courtyard when the tidal wave of stagnant rain water reached her. The washing basket surfed off as the water swished around her legs and splashed up her skirt.

'Christ almighty,' she shrieked. 'What the bloody hell's going on, ya stupid buggers!'

Having soon realised the situation, Micky ran for the yard broom. Wielding it around like a Claymore, she chased us down the driveway shouting not to come back unless we'd bought another rain butt.

I tried my key in the front door for about the ninth time that night and this time it opened. It was 1.30am and I had no barrel. Kenny came home from a tour that weekend and Micky had arranged an inquest into the barrel incident. Replacement value, pocket money, lawn mowing and window cleaning were all discussed.

'Right, I'll go and get a new barrel at Roxeth Nurseries,' said Kenny. 'Jeremy, come with me, I'll need a hand'.

We found a barrel and somehow jammed it into the boot of the Daimler by forcing the boot lid open further than it should and then we drove two hundred yards to the Black Horse pub. I went and sat in the beer garden and Kenny came back with a Guinness for him and a shandy for me. He ripped open a bag of crisps and looked me right in the eye.

'Right' he said. 'So how does this firework thing work then?'

Kenny appeared in a total of seventeen of the thirty-one *Carry On* films. Indeed, after *Carry On Up the Jungle*, apart for an appearance in the Eric Sykes silent 1970 silent film, *Rhubarb*, all of his big-screen appearances were with the *Carry On* team. He can also be seen in several clips featured in the 1977 compilation film, *That's Carry On!*

The full list of *Carry On* films which Kenny appeared in is as follows:

Carry On Sergeant
Carry On Nurse
Carry On Teacher
Carry On Constable
Carry On Regardless
Carry On Cruising
Carry On Cabby

Carry On Cleo
Carry On Up the Jungle
Carry On Henry
Carry On Matron
Carry On Abroad
Carry On Girls
Carry On Dick
Carry On Behind
Carry On England
Carry On Emmannuelle.

Kenny still wanted to be a dramatic actor, and at the height of his *Carry On* fame he would get very depressed claiming, quite wrongly, that he was a failure. It took a long time for him to come to terms with the position he was in, a position that many actors would, ironically, have envied! Not all of Kenny's film roles were part of the *Carry On* series, of course. But if one looks at his film credits, it's obvious that his ability as a talented comedy actor inspired producers to continue to cast him in other comedy titles. They included *Make Mine a Million*, *Watch Your Stern*, *Dentist in the Chair*, *Nearly a Nasty Accident*, *A Weekend with Lulu*, *Dentist on the Job*, *What a Carve Up!* and *Cuckoo Patrol*. But even then, many of these films included his colleagues from the *Carry On* films.

Kenny did have his ups and downs with the *Carry On* team members, just like in any family, but he loved working with nearly all of them. They had great fun filming the series, and whatever you have heard about their pranks is true. Director Gerald Thomas said there was more footage on the cutting room floor, through corpsing and ad-libs, than was out in the cinema. They were a happy band, and no more united than when they whinged about their salaries! For instance, there was the time when some of the team were sitting in a coach at Pinewood, and the producer, Peter Rogers, walked by smiling and waving at them and blowing kisses. From his point of view all his stars were smiling and waving back, but if you had been on board the bus it was a different story. Through forced smiles, truths were hissed out.

'Never mind all that lovey dovey shit,' said Kenneth Williams 'Where`s the fucking money?!'

'Yes, you tight fucker', added Joan Sims.

Meanwhile, the rest all joined in the abuse. Well, it got it out of their systems for a while!

In his first film, *Carry On Sergeant*, which was released in 1958, Kenny played the role of Horace Strong. Horace was an incompetent private who wanted to fall in love, but did not have the courage. My parents had talked about the idea of him appearing in this film at great length. At the time, they wondered whether it would it be damaging to his radio career, especially as he was just becoming a household name. Believe it or not, they even considered whether the public would want to see his face!

I saw Kenny every night when he was making *Carry On Sergeant*. The six week schedule had very strict shooting times and a tight budget. This meant he was able to spend time with me, and getting Home Oaks up and running. Well, not quite, because Kenny still had radio commitments and was working pretty well seven days a week. But he managed because he loved his trade.

Carry On Nurse followed very quickly, and I got my first acting role! It was nothing too challenging – I played Kenny's son. I was only three! Four guineas was the fee, which paid for lunch at Pinewood Studios and a cab back home with Micky – so she said!

The Connor family have always been prolific swearers, especially my grandad. Kenny always said that swear words have saved many a murder! So there's this tale that goes around the *Carry On* fraternity about getting little Jeremy to perform his piece in *Carry On Nurse*. The scene in question was where my character greeted his professional boxer father, Bernie Bishop, in hospital just as he was being discharged with a broken hand. Kenny had rehearsed me every night after I had taken a bath. The words were simple and went something along the lines of:

'Hello Jeremy. Have you got something for me?'
'Yes.'

With that, I was supposed to give him a right hook on his jaw. However, on the actual day I gave him a left hook and he fell over. Not bad for a three-year-old!

Gerald Thomas once claimed in a radio interview that he said to me if I did another take just the same, then there would be some Mars Bars behind the camera for me. His version went as follows:

'Hello Jeremy, have you got something for me?'
'Yes, but there's some Mars Bars behind the camera for me.'

However, it wasn't Mars Bars, it was a trolley of wooden building bricks. And, for the record, what I actually said was:

'Yes, but where's my bloody bricks?!'

I know it's only a small thing but that's the way our relationship grew.

On the 14 March 1974, I had lunch with both Kenny and Kenneth Williams at Pinewood Studios while we were working on *Carry On Dick*. Williams recalled the time I was taken to Pinewood to film my appearance in *Carry On Nurse*. I was pleased to discover many years later that Kenneth had recorded this lunch in his famous diary. And while not everybody was mentioned favourably in his diaries, which were edited by Russell Davies, and first published in 1993, I was lucky. He actually described me as, '…a good-looking and sensitive boy'.

I was amused to read recently that the censor made a certain request prior to granting *Carry On Nurse* a certificate. It appears that they took exception to the original ending that screenplay writer, Norman Hudis, wrote for the scene, in which the two nurses removed Kenny's underwear. After declaring that he, as Bernie Bishop, was making a lot of fuss about 'such a little thing', Kenny was originally meant to look rather put out as he glanced under the sheets. But the latter shot had to be removed from the sequence at the request of the censor. How times and attitudes have changed in the UK!

Actress Shirley Eaton, who appeared in three *Carry On* films, including *Carry On Nurse*, and other comedy films with Kenny, including *Dentist on the Job*, still has positive memories of the actor:

'I really liked Kenneth, but he wasn't funny off-screen, like Kenneth Williams and Joan Sims. He stood out as he didn't look like an actor, and he was not very theatrical. In fact, he was shy and very real. He was genuine – which is a quality I admire. I would have liked to have got to know him more, but there wasn't time when we were on set.'

The next *Carry On* film Kenny appeared in was *Carry On Teacher*. Released in 1959, it featured Kenny's radio colleague, Ted Ray, in his one and only *Carry On* film role.

Kenny played the role of nervous science master, Gregory Adams, a man whose unique charms are noticed by one of the Ministry of Education inspector, Felicity Wheeler (Rosalind Knight).

As well as the usual cast members of the time being present in the line-up, including Charles Hawtrey and Hattie Jacques, a young Richard O'Sullivan played one of the school boys, Robin Stevens.

Carry On Constable, which first hit cinema screens in 1960, was made when the scripts were great for the actor to work with. You may remember the famous scene in the film where Kenny, Kenneth Williams, Charles Hawtrey and Leslie Philips had to bare their bums for the camera. When director Gerald Thomas informed them that they would have to have make-up applied to their bums, which were apparently flaring under the studio lights, Leslie Philips wasn't exactly over the moon at Thomas' solution to the problem.

'Look, Leslie,' signed Kenny. 'The films are on the way up, audiences are up, and the takings are up, so get your bum made up!'

Location filming for *Carry On Constable* also brought another memorable moment for Kenny when a child asked him for his autograph.

'Hang on a minute – I'm being directed,' replied Kenny.

'Oh, are you lost then?' asked the child.

Just to clarify, the little boy who goes missing in the film, and finally comes back home to his mother (played by Irene Handl) on a scooter, was not played by me. Some people have claimed on the internet that it is me! But I'm afraid it's just another one of those famous *Carry On* legends that seems to have got around. Although I will be honest and admit that I was asked to do the small non-speaking role. Although, for some reason that eludes me now, I stubbornly said no!

Kenny was soon back with the *Carry On* team again, this time to play the role of Sam Twist in the 1961 film, *Carry On Regardless*.

Arguably, one of his most memorable scenes in *Regardless* saw Kenny playing opposite Fenella Fielding, who was playing Mrs. Panting, a lady who desperately wanted to make her husband jealous. Twist had been booked through an agency called Helping Hands. This was on the understanding that he would be doing a spot of babysitting. Despite actually succeeding in making Panting's husband jealous, Twist unfortunately gets knocked-out by Mr. Panting in return for his efforts!

There were memorable scenes opposite another actress in the 1962 comedy, *Carry On Cruising*. This time, Kenny played Arthur Binn, a cruise ship doctor who falls for the delectable Flo Castle, played by Dilys Laye. At first, Castle seems intent on marrying practically every man she sets her eyes upon at first, including the ship's captain, Captain Wellington Crowther, played by Sid James. But in the end it is Binn who manages to woo the previously uninterested holiday-maker.

June 1963, saw cinema-goers treated to the *Carry On* team in *Carry On Cabby*. Sid James played Charlie Hawkins, a work obsessed owner of a busy taxi company, while Kenny played his best mate and colleague, Ted Watson.

Kenny did not appear in the following two *Carry On* films – *Jack* and *Spying* – due to his work-load and his desire to try different projects. However, he was destined to return for the 1964 film, *Carry On Cleo*.

Chapter Four

Kenny's Jolly Holidays And Pranks

Kenny loved travelling but hated hotels, hotel culture and the formalities that went along with it. He also abhorred any sort of queues, crowded beaches and vast dining rooms. Oh, and he hated tourists, especially German ones! So you may be wondering why Kenny started taking his family on package holidays? Simple! He wanted to show them around a bit. Micky had never been abroad and neither had little Jeremy. The war had shown Kenny many countries and he told these recollections to his wife. Micky had become intrigued and keen to experience some of these places for herself.

By the mid-Fifties, travelling abroad for holidays had become quite the thing to do, and there were companies willing to arrange it all for you! So off we went!

Portugal was the first experience, and the year was 1959. The destination was Foz do Arelho, north of Lisbon. It must have been a totally 'out of the way' place in those days. And as I was only three at the time, I can't remember much of this experience. I can, however, remember the large Atlantic roller formed sand banks that Kenny and I would run at and slide down. Massive, almost vertical walls of sand that seemed like the height of a London double-decker bus to my three year-old self. There were trips to Porto for the Port and Fatima for the Virgin Mary, plus Lisbon for the architecture and beautiful Portuguese leather goods.

Kenny enjoyed the peace and simple peasant style living at the beach, where no-one knew who he was. Word did, somehow, reach the hotel management that the Englishman was a celebrity in his country, but they really did not know why. One morning, while at reception, he was told that a famous Portuguese celebrity lived in the village and that they would like Señor Connor to meet him. Kenny was on the verge of declining when it was explained that this celebrity was a bull fighter, and so he jumped at the suggestion. It was arranged to meet in the hotel foyer that evening before dinner time.

When we arrived at the agreed time that evening, the Matador was standing in the middle of the marble reception hall talking to the manager. He was not tall, but athletic and swarthy with a mass of pitch black curly hair. He was dressed in a white suit with an open-collar shirt, and a Panama hat held in one hand. Micky never forgot this sight. She would often tell of Bruno the Matador!

With introductions completed, we went to the terrace for drinks which Bruno bought. He insisted they must have the Vinho Verde. Kenny fell in love with this young, robust white wine and often had bottles of it in his bar at home. Kenny asked him what it was like to be a bullfighter, and in broken English Bruno said that it was not like Spanish bull fighting where you always kill the bull.

'In Portugal it was a game with the bull,' he explained. 'You play with the bull, you make laughs and make fun with the bull'.

Micky was loving this idea and this matador was now a saint! But in fact, they took the poor bull out the back and killed it. The village butcher then took over and there was a village hand out! But it varies on which league you are in. In premier league, the kill happens in the arena, just like in Spain, but as you go down the leagues, the less of a lavish opera it becomes, until you end up with a panto where the matador is the Prince Charming and the supporting cast all wear funny hats and costumes and tumble over the bull like The Acromaniacs. It also transpired that Bruno was not only a matador, but also of the Forcados (a troupe of eight men who do tumbling tricks).

At the end of the meeting, Bruno had decided to be the personal guide for Señor Connor's family as he really wanted to 'show them the real Portuguese life'. He picked us up in the morning after breakfast. Micky was ecstatic.

'By, wor, Ken, a real matador givin' us a grand tour!' she exclaimed.

But when our matador turned up to take us sight-seeing, it was not in the black Mercedes that Micky had imagined, it was really Coco the Clown in a Bubble Car!! Yes, a real Bubble Car. An Isetta made by BMW. We all crammed in with me on the parcel shelf and apparently a fun, sweaty day was had by all. We were taken to meet Bruno's family and friends for a traditional lunch. There, we were served with freshly caught sardines that were brought up from a boat on the beach. They had simple salad and boiled potatoes and Vinho Verde with breads and fruits. Kenny was in his element and this was just his style.

In the afternoon, we were taken to the bullring to watch a team training session – just like football see! They were practising a grappling technique with young bulls and tumbling over their backs and all the time the wine flowed. Now that was the sort of holiday that Kenny loved. He liked hanging around with the locals and not the hotels. Most of the other ventures abroad were unremarkable, resort style living and coach tours which went along with autographs and boring unsolicited conversations. For those reasons alone, I won't mention these – except for the following few stories!

Ibiza, 1960: Full scale tourism was in its infancy and airlines could not fly there direct. We changed planes at Madrid and flew into Ibiza on an overhead winged part cargo plane. It had a fixed undercarriage and landed on an unmade runway in a field where large stones flew up and pelted the fuselage. The luggage was thrown out on to the ground and you just picked out your own cases. The hotel was spartan and you had to cross an open sewer to get to the beach. The hotel had a food shortage and the residents lived mainly on green tomato and onion salad.

One day, the three goats that the tourist children petted in the field next door disappeared and grey chicken was on the menu that night. Yes, it was like something out of *Carry On Abroad*! One-time *Doctor Who* actor, Jon Pertwee, told Kenny to visit to his bar in Ibiza town – but it was still very much under construction!

Portugal, 1968: Our hotel was in a small fishing village halfway between Albufeira and Portimao. It had a rooftop restaurant with wide views over the sea and amazing sunsets. Kenny enjoyed anonymity for the first week, with a beautiful unspoilt beach to wander on. All that was there were fishing boats, a large tin shed that was used for repairing nets, and a fabulous beach bar built into the cliff.

Kenny had bought a small telescope with us and we would go down to the beach each night and set it up on an upturned fishing boat and gaze at the moon. This brought out all the village kids who would queue up to have a look at the telescope, bringing gasps of amazement and squeals of joy. It took ages for us to get a turn!

One day the tin shed was emptied out and seats were carried in. Out of curiosity, we asked what was going on.

'Tonight is cinema night,' a man informed us.

This happened once a week. The next morning there was a crowd outside the hotel entrance standing quietly and seemed to be waiting for something. The kids had realised that 'the telescope man' was in the movie! Believe it or not, they had shown *Carry On Sergeant* in the tin shed! Kenny went to see them and all they wanted to do was see him and smile and shake his hand. No autographs were requested. Kenny found this refreshing, and he was not hassled – except for the telescope!

Denmark (again in the Sixties): A strange choice with a young child? It rained the whole time and even the cinema was visited. We went to see *South Pacific* and little me was so impressed by the musical that in the interval I stood on my seat and sang 'My Old Man`s A Dustman'. I couldn't have been that bad as I was showered with Kroner coins!

Later in the week, Kenny decided to take a look at the waterfront. Micky did not want to trail around with me, so went off to find a café. When Kenny eventually found us, we were sitting inside a café brothel and the proprietor had been trying desperately to get us to leave as it was killing their trade! Micky had insisted that I needed feeding, and so a bowl of soup was placed in front of me. The Madam spooned it down me quickly so they could get rid of us! Realising where we were, Kenny frantically called us from the doorway to a waiting taxi.

Cyprus, 1967: Kenny went back to war – this time taking his family with him! Two weeks before the holiday there was a two-hour pitched battle between the

Greeks and the Turks on this already troubled island, and when we landed at Athens we had to change from BEA to Cyprus Airlines. Our plane was surrounded by tanks and armed soldiers. After a long wait, while they changed the plane's signage from BEA to Cyprus Airlines, we were finally able to continue with our journey.

When we arrived in Nicosia, we were told by our personal agent representative that we could not travel to our hotel in the north of the island as all travel was at a halt. It had been arranged that we should stay at the Hilton Hotel in the city. We were taken to the hotel there in a large Mercedes which drove through many road blocks made of upturned trucks and there we stayed in this business hotel full of diplomats. It was like being in a *James Bond* film with all these suited embassy sorts standing in small covert huddles drinking Martinis, while looking over their shoulders. There were many Arabs there in their flowing robes and Rolexes, which added to the excitement. Dinner time must have looked funny with this small tourist family sticking out like a sore thumb! One diplomat came over and introduced himself.

'Are you here to entertain the troops, Mr. Connor?' he asked.

The United Nations troops were here in force, and when we did make it to our destination hotel in Kyrenia there were Scout Ferret armoured vehicles on the streets and beaches. This did not deter Kenny's family. We trusted him! I thought it was a great adventure, being an eleven-year-old! There were no beaches on this part of the coastline, so the hotel sourced a local hire car for us, a Ford Zodiac V4, with column change gears. The car was a heap with a split right through the interior of the vehicle from the transmission tunnel to the dashboard.

It constantly backfired which caused dogs to try and bite the tread off the tyres as we drove through the villages and lemon groves to the beach. Kenny renamed the car The Sodiac!

Six-and-a-Half-Mile Beach was so named by the UN troops as it was six-and-a-half-miles from somewhere or other. The beach was fabulously clean and there was a Greek run café bar high up on the cliff to one side of the beach. It had a gun emplacement facing out to sea and bullet holes through the railings of the veranda. If you told the owners that you wanted lunch at noon, they'd ring a bell to call you up from the beach.

One day, an armoured car screamed down on to the beach and the crew jumped out and ran into the sea to cool down. When they tried to leave they got stuck in the sand and they had to radio ahead for help! It took another three Scout Ferrets to tow it out! They obviously had no idea how to handle these machines. My Matchbox version never got stuck!

There was a flea-pit cinema in Kyrenia, which Kenny could not resist going to as it was always full of troops. We saw *Jason and the Argonauts*. The film had so many different language subtitles on the screen that you could hardly make out the action! In a way, this strange holiday allowed Kenny to show his family how he had spent his army life in the Middle East during the war.

Several weeks after this holiday, on 12 October 1967, flight 284, a Cyprus Airline flight operated and serviced by BEA, and was a Comet, blew up en route from Athens to Nicosia. Traces of military explosives were found.

The last straw for Kenny and tourist holidays was the Canary Isles. He had booked a five star hotel in Las Palmas, Gran Canaria. On the flight there, he had scolding hot coffee poured in his lap. And when we went down to the hotel dining room, he was told he had to wear a tie for dinner. He never went down for dinner again! Instead, while we ate, he would go outside with a suitcase and fill it with stones from a building site and take it back to our room. He would then carry it out on to the balcony and throw the stones at the bull frogs in the stagnant pond by the building site, while drinking duty free whisky. He spent the rest of his holidays sailing in the South of France on his best mate's boat. Captain Alan Lane and First Officer Kenny all at sea!!

Back in 1962, Kenny returned to the theatre after a few years break and appeared in a revue at the Duke of York's theatre called *One Over the Eight*. He took over a role previously played by his *Carry On* colleague, Kenneth Williams.

Later, Kenny appeared on stage with the much-loved comedian, Frankie Howerd, in a successful two-year run of the musical, *A Funny Thing Happened on the Way to the Forum*. He loved the musical and the cast, but could not tolerate Howerd's work ethic. Kenny would complain that Howerd did not know how to act within a cast and within a play. Worse still, the two men simply didn't get on. They feuded in the wings, in the corridors and dressing rooms. Kenny's blood was boiling and Frankie knew which buttons to press. This ended in them coming to blows on several occasions and required one of the creators, Burt Shevelove, to fly in from the States to sort it out. They were both threatened with the sack if they did not pack it in. There was a bad undercurrent between them that carried on, which I can personally vouch for.

I used to go to the theatre some nights with Kenny when Micky was out and a babysitter could not be found. I suppose it might seem odd to some for an eight-year-old to be hanging around in theatres and restaurants until midnight, but it was just natural for me.

One particular night, I went into the wings to watch, and when Kenny went on stage, Frankie whispered to me to come and sit with him to keep out of the way. He pulled me onto his knee and held me tight to his sweating body. The costumes that Kenny and Frankie wore looked great, but were made of wool that made them sweat and itch under the heat of the lights! Frankie squeezed me tighter and then pinched my leg in a firm grip.

'Your daddy hates me, doesn't he?' he said.

Just then, Kenny came off stage and came over to get me. Frankie then went straight onstage. I never told Kenny this or it would have caused yet another row! I imagine Peter Rogers and Gerald Thomas must have kept a close eye on the two of them when they worked together again on *Carry On Up the Jungle*.

Apart from the Connor v Howerd aspect, Kenny loved the two years he spent on the show. The cast also included Jon Pertwee, Robertson Hare, Linda Gray, Leon Greene and the devilish 'Monsewer' Eddie Gray, who definitely coloured Kenny's life.

Thursdays were matinee days and in between shows it became a regular habit for Kenny and Eddie to eat in a nearby Italian restaurant, off The Strand. One week, Eddie said he would meet Kenny in the restaurant as he had to go and do something first. He sat there having ordered for both of them. After waiting for what seemed like an eternity, Kenny suddenly heard a commotion at the front of the café. And there was Eddie, with a large post office sack, making his way through crowded tables bumping into them and apologising to the customers as he went.

'What have you got there, eh, Eddie?' said a waiter.

'Fan mail son, fan mail,' replied Eddie, reaching Kenny and making a huge palaver of trying to stuff the sack under the table.

'What are you up to Eddie?' Kenny asked.

'I hate getting fan mail, I really do,' he said. 'Now where's the grub? I don't want to hang around here too long.'

Eddie was speaking in a loud voice and behaving very agitatedly, glancing over his shoulder this way and that. The pasta arrived and Eddie made a big show of eating his spaghetti, slurping and sucking on each mouthful. His behaviour was now the centre of attention in the room and Kenny thought he would just stay quiet and see what the scam was.

The meal over, Kenny paid the bill while Eddie struggled with his sack.

'You go first Kenneth and stay close!' said Eddie, again a loud voice.

They set off through the restaurant.

'Did you leave a tip?' asked Eddie.

Kenny replied that he had. Eddie glancing at the table.

'That's not enough, you tight bastard!' he replied loudly.

Eddie headed back to the table, dragging the sack. He delved his arm into it and pulled out a five pound note, shook it out above his head and examined it before placing it onto the table. Now that was a huge tip in those days and, of course, was noticed. Eddie now picked up the sack and started heading back to the entrance. Five pound notes started falling from the bottom of the sack scattering on the floor.

'Shit,' exclaimed Eddie. 'We've been rumbled, run for it!'

62

And with that, they bundled out of the door and ran around the corner to the stage door leaving the restaurant in mayhem.

This was the year of 'The Great Train Robbery' and was on everyone's mind. An expensive practical joke, yes, but what clever planning, and Eddie got his result and most of his fivers back actually! Kenny wanted to know why Eddie had gone to such great lengths to do this. Eddie explained that as part of The Crazy Gang (he was one of the founder members of this pioneering comedy group) they had all been outdoing each other with outrageous pranks and it was still going on.

One of the other members of The Crazy Gang had pulled a stunt at another Italian restaurant in London only the previous week. This restaurant was a favourite haunt of the Gang and when the Crazy had rung late in the day he was told it was full. He knew this was a fib and possibly they didn't want mad cap follies at the end of the day. But, they would have to pay for this! The café style eatery was a small, one room affair with a door leading off directly to the only toilet. A mate was employed for this scam and sent into the restaurant on a busy lunch session, complaining that he did not feel well and asked to use the loo. He entered the toilet, leaving the door wide open and having put a plug in the sink tipped a diluted can of Heinz vegetable salad (that was concealed under his coat and hung round his neck on string) into it while making loud vomit sounds. He then made his excuses and left the shocked people. A minute lapsed and in came the Crazy.

'Has my mate been in here?' asked the performer.

'He's not well, you know.' He was told.

The staff explained to him what had happened in a very animated fashion while the diners sat uncomfortably, not eating.

'I'll sort it out,' said the Crazy.

The comedian then took a large spoon out of his jacket pocket he went into the loo and started spooning the 'vomit' into his mouth. Well, that was it! The restaurant emptied and the Crazy slowly emerged from the loo.

'Can I book a table for this evening, as long as you're not full?' he asked.

It was a wicked scam and, again, expensive, as all the unpaid tabs were paid in full.

Kenny decided to try a simple practical joke first. Mate, his father, had not yet seen *A Funny Thing Happened on the Way to the Forum*, saying it would be wasted on him due to his partial deafness. Kenny saw a new type of hearing aid that was a microphone receiver about the size of a small transistor radio and an ear piece on a cable. It could be worn in various ways, including on a jacket breast pocket. With this bought and tried out, Mate came to a midweek matinee and after the show he and his actor son went for a stroll before Mate caught a train home. They had a pint and discussed the merits of the hearing aid.

'It was a different experience,' he told his son. 'I could hear everything. The band was so clear and I could hear all the sods that were coughing.'

'Great,' said Kenny.

The two men then walked over Waterloo Bridge. They stopped in the middle to gaze up the river towards Parliament. It was the middle of the rush hour and noisy with traffic. Kenny quickly turned up the volume on the hearing aid which, not surprisingly, made Mate jump out of his skin.

'You little bastard!' he yelled.

Kenny jumped on a slow moving bus, leaving Mate to sort himself out.

When Kenny got home that night, Micky had left out the usual cold plate of meats and salad for him. He went into the bar to get a beer. He and Mate used to drink large brown quart bottles of Watneys Pale Ale, buying it by the crate and splitting it. He saw that there was only one left. Funny, he thought. Had Mate run out and taken some across the road to his house? He grabbed a tankard, unscrewed the stopper and poured it. It was full of cold milky tea, so the prank feud started in earnest!

A Funny Thing... was the most-favourite musical that Kenny undertook in his career. But I do remember that there was a particular aspect of the show which annoyed him. As you may or may not know, a 'cod routine' is where you pretend to the audience that something has gone wrong and pretend that you're having to control your laughter. Kenny hated doing these, as he thought gaining laughs this way was cheating. In one part of the production he had to dress up as a Vestal Virgin – complete with a veil and a long black wig! It was written into the script that his wig had to get caught up before being pulled off by another actor. The two actors had to pretend to conceal fake laughs while turning up stage to fumble the wig back in place before resuming the action. Kenny did this every night for two years and it never failed to get huge laughs.

Kenny was excited to be asked to direct a tour of *A Funny Thing...* after the West End run ended. Charles Hawtrey was cast in dad's role, and Kenny would travel to the show once a week to oversee it and give the cast notes, if he felt it was appropriate. Yet when Kenny guested on *Desert Island Discs*, and Roy Plomley asked him if he'd ever had any ambitions to direct for the stage, he replied:

'No, no I never have had. Always thought it would be impertinent for me to tell established artistes what to do!'

Kenny's next *Carry On* role, which would be his last for a number of years, was to give me the opportunity to get to know Pinewood Studios a little better.

Chapter Five

Carrying On

It was seven o'clock on a glorious early August morning in 1964 when Kenny pulled up at the lodge gates of Pinewood Studios in his silver blue Jaguar MK2 240. I was sitting alongside him, very excited. We were there for the shooting of *Carry On Cleo*. It was my first time at Pinewood since I was a toddler on *Carry On Nurse*. A security guard came over to greet us.

'Good morning, Mr. Connor,' he said, as he waved us through.

Pinewood is such a magical place, a real 'Dream Factory'. The studios are built in the massive grounds of a Victorian country house, which is used as an administration block. Some dressing rooms and the main make-up rooms are housed there too. It also contains the fabulous wood panelled bar and restaurant.

Kenny drove us to his parking bay marked 'Kenneth Connor' and we went straight to make up. The room was already buzzing with 'good mornings' all round. He sat in a chair and the preparation started. Just as the make-up artist was finishing, the runner came in to say that there had been a change to the shooting order, and Kenny wouldn't be needed until about ten-thirty. Ah well, that's filming for you!

With time to kill, Kenny decided to take me for a look around his place of work.

'Come on, let's explore!' he said excitedly. 'But first, breakfast'.

There was a large heated serving trolley with a waitress standing behind. The crew were all lining up and walking away with filled rolls. All sorts of hot rolls were on offer with delicious fillings, including scrambled eggs, bacon, bacon and mushroom, sausage, you name it. Kenny took two bacon rolls and put tomato sauce in mine. This reminds me that the actress Linda Regan mentioned recently that Kenny once confided in her about my obsession with red sauce.

'Jeremy puts so much tomato sauce on his morning bacon sarnies that I'm surprised he doesn't have red hair!' he said grinning.

Having grabbed our breakfast, we went back into the sun, through the old mansion house and out of some French windows onto the most splendid lawns. There was a huge ornamental pond with an ornate stone bridge spanning it. We stood at the edge eating our rolls and sprinkling the crumbs on the water to attract the large carp.

Kenny then led me to the end of the lake, where there was a large rock wall. He led me behind the wall and into a cave. It was cool and damp with a stone bench built on one side and an opening to look out over the water. All amazing for an eight year-old, of course!

Coming out of the cave we walked through large rhododendron shrubs and out onto the back lot, and there in front of us was another sort of pond, all concrete and above ground level. Behind it was a massively wide and tall canvas painted to look like the sky. Sitting on the surface of the water was a large accurate model of a World War Two warship.

'Is that a swimming pool?' I asked.

'No,' Kenny laughed. 'At the moment it's the North Atlantic.'

It was what in those days they called a panorama tank. It could make waves and when carefully filmed it could look like the high seas. We moved on and entered a Mexican village, just like on the Westerns. Kenny told me it was a set being used for *The Saint*. Remember that series with Roger Moore? However, *The Saint* was filmed at Elstree Studios, and I think he just said that to excite me as I loved that show and Roger Moore was my hero! It was Kenny embellishing again!

We carried on looking around the back of a studio, and there in front of us was a Victorian Baker Street. This of course had been built for *Sherlock Holmes*. This was stunning, even for grown-ups! It was time to head back.

Kenny and I went into the studio where it was bustling. Lights were being moved and the camera was being repositioned. Gerald Thomas spotted Kenny and came over clutching his leather script file under his arm and greeted us both. He apologised for the delay, saying they would be ready in five minutes.

Kenny showed me around some of the sets. They were stunning compared to other *Carry On* productions so far. I didn't fancy hanging around while the filming was going on, I was a bit young for what is a very slow process.

'Dad, can I go outside for another look around?' I asked eagerly.

I was desperate to get back to my new found playground.

'Okay son, be safe and be back by half-past-twelve as lunch is always prompt,' he ordered. 'And don't come back onto the set if the red light is on outside the studio door. Wait until you hear a bell and the red light goes green.'

I was out! I ran straight round to the Mexican village and played cowboys – well, John Wayne actually – shooting out the baddies from behind walls. Then I cantered up Baker Street on my horse.

Time flew by and when I next looked at my school boy Timex watch, it was half-past-twelve, so I ran back and the light was green on the studio door. I tugged on the heavy, soundproofed door and managed to open it just as the bell rang and the red light came on. I crept in and stood in the dark of the back wall away from the set. I could hear Kenny delivering a line as his character, Hengis Pod. He did it three times and all I remember is that it contained his famous 'Cor!'

'Right, that's this scene done, great work and thanks Kenny,' said Gerald. 'Let's reset for the first scene after lunch and then take a break.'

Kenny was released and came to find me. 'Right, lunch,' he said. 'I'm bloody starving.'

We went to wardrobe and an assistant helped Kenny out of his armour and uniform and off we went to the restaurant. He told me that we were having lunch with Kenneth Williams, and we met him there at a table.

'Oh, there you are!' wined Kenneth. 'I've been bloody waiting for you! Here's the boring menu.'

Well, it was the Sixties in England and gourmet was not really in the language then. So different now! I know I had fish and chips and peas and all the way through the meal Kenneth kept us entertained. Kenny and I laughed so much at his banter. Obviously a lot of it went over my head, but it was a great experience. He told me I should always eat my peas off a knife. Wow, my grandad had taught me that. I was warming to this man. Every time I offered up my knife of peas to tip into my mouth Kenneth would come up with a one-liner and I would be spitting peas all over the table.

Presently, a waitress came over to our table with a jug.

'Would you like some more water?' she asked helpfully.

'No,' said Kenneth with his trademark delivery. 'We've been poisoned enough already, thank you!' he joked

After lunch, Kenny got back in costume and went for a make-up check before we were back on set. Gerald Thomas said I could stand beside him by the camera and watch what happened. I can't remember the scene, but even at that early stage in life I learnt some filming techniques. Starting on a wide shot filming the whole scene and then going in for two shots and then singles. This was a great gesture from Gerald and it served me well decades later. What a family team the *Carry On* films were. However, the cast, as I mentioned earlier, did have one or two reservations about producer, Peter Rogers.

Kenny was finished by four o'clock and we went home. He had bought me some aviator goggles from the army surplus store in South Harrow Market. I would sit in the back seat of the Jag and he would pull back the sun roof then I would stand on the transmission tunnel with goggles on with my head out of the roof, doing a hundred miles an hour down the Western Avenue!

Micky greeted us at home and was getting an early dinner ready, as Kenny had to go up to the West End to perform in *A Funny Thing Happened on the Way to the Forum*. He was working very hard, but loving it, even with the internal politics of the *Carry On* films. He tried to steer away from that side of things and simply enjoy the job.

Sundays might have given Kenny a rest from the film studio, but there was usually some radio comedy or other to be recorded for the BBC at the Playhouse Theatre on Northumberland Avenue. Firstly, there would be the Sunday lunch roast and an afternoon kip for Kenny, who would doze on a goat skin rug in front of the log fire with some old war movie on the TV. Then it was off to the theatre for the recording, and often we would go as a family. There was a tradition that the artistes used to go to the nearby Sherlock Holmes pub for a few after show drinks. It was always a relaxed and a fun forty-minutes or so, and then everyone would fade into the night, having had a wonderful finish to the weekend.

In late 1968, Kenny was offered a part in an MGM fantasy-adventure film, which boasted a crop of British and Hollywood stars. Entitled *Captain Nemo and the Underwater City*, the film starred Robert Ryan and Chuck Connors, Luciana Paluzzi and Nanette Newman, Bill Fraser and Kenneth Connor. The film was shot at the since-demolished MGM Studios in Borehamwood. Ryan was Nemo, Connors, the hero and Kenny and Bill, the comedy robbers. Kenny had great fun filming this one – apart from the hours of being freezing cold while immersed in water tanks on the sound stage for all those underwater scenes! Chuck Connors was 6ft 5" tall and Kenny pushing 5ft 6". They soon became known on the set as Chuck and Chick!!

During the filming, there was a traditional Christmas dinner with mince pies and crackers that was laid on for the rest of the cast and crew. But I can't recall if it was held in honour of Christmas or Thanksgiving! Anyway, when the mince pies were being handed around, Bill Fraser put his false teeth under the pastry top of one, making sure Robert Ryan received it!

Whenever I had girlfriend trouble, Kenny used to tell me that the heart leads you up an often hurtful track. And when I had to prepare for my first divorce, it was Kenny set up the legal side for me. He took me to my godfather, Christopher Bywaters, a madcap man and probably the best godfather you could ever wish for!

We had been neighbours when we lived in Hemington Avenue, Friern Barnet and was a very close friend of ours. Kenny was very concerned that I was not seeing another girl at the time as it could be financially disastrous. He was fearful of this. It puzzled me. My godfather endorsed Kenny's fears.

'Yes, Jeremy, abstain from carnal knowledge,' he advised. 'We better get this done and dusted before the ugly beast raises its head again!'

The separation from the fun loving Helen had been a hurtful experience, but that's normal, and we had a simple fifty-fifty split of limited funds. There had been no one else involved in the first place, and went our separate ways having married way to young.

I was confused at Kenny's paranoid attitude to my divorce. It was stupid because I knew he'd had an affair ten years before hand, in 1970, with a lady who, for the purposes of this book, I will call Shirley. Shirley was approximately half of Kenny's age. She was an extremely attractive singer and dancer who also did hand modelling and was sometimes a lingerie model. I'm not sure how or where they met, but she soon became part of the family. Kenny introduced her as this struggling singer he was trying to help. Micky got on with Shirley famously as they both came from the same background in Northumberland. She would come over during the week to rehearse at Home Oaks and soon came to every Sunday lunch.

Being a thirteen-year-old lad at the time, I soon had great interest in Shirley, and her trendy, flash Morris Mini Minor and her micro mini-skirts and tights with a flash of floral knickers! Even my girlfriend, Annie, liked her and Shirley loved watching me flying down South Hill Avenue on my Chopper bike with Annie sitting behind me, her long blonde hair flowing back in the wind. This inspired her to say once, 'By, ya look dead romantic'.

Shirley lived with her parents in Hounslow and we received an invite to come over. She explained that her folks were getting a bit miffed that she wasn`t around for Sunday lunch with them, hence the invite. So we duly went and Micky got on really well with them. They had both been in hotel service and it was like being back in 'Geordie land', with me and Kenny being the only southerners. The families grew even closer, with Christmas Day being celebrated at both houses. For Kenny, everything revolved around Shirley. It was during one particular day out on Kenny's boat (which I will tell you about later!) when I finally discovered that this friendship was also an affair.

By now, I was fifteen and had started to feel I was a man of experience, what with being in a serious relationship with my girlfriend, Annie. We`d even talked of marriage! I was also at that age when you wonder whether your parents still 'do it' and then immediately chased that thought away with a shudder! Kenny and Micky always had those large single beds in the master bedroom at Home Oaks, but now they had separate bedrooms, this being explained as due to Kenny`s snoring. Armed with this knowledge of their sleeping arrangements, and my worldly experience, I did not react to this shock revelation. I sagely knew that a man has his needs, oh yes!

On the day of the confirmation of the affair we – Kenny, Micky, Shirley and I – had partaken of a good lunch at the Kings Arms in Cookham village. We'd strolled back through a meadow to the river bank near to Kenny's boat, the John Francis, where we all plonked down for a sun bathe. I was laying on my front with Micky to my right, Kenny to my left and Shirley beyond him. We were just passing the time of day when I turned my head to the left and saw Shirley's delicate model's hand shoved down the front of Kenny's swim shorts and moving oh so slowly. The Pond's hand cream advert immediately jumped into the teenage mind. The true image, though, was now in my photographic memory. Some thoughts fled through my mind as I turned my head away. One of them being, I can't blame him, it's a man's needs – I would have! But bloody hell, Shirley! I was naturally more vigilant of them both after that and found them in desperate and sad embraces at Home Oaks on a number of occasions. They weren't happy. Kenny crying and Shirley stroking his hair. Shirley spotted me once and came to find me after a while. She said we should go for a walk. So we went up to Orley Farm School fields and sat down on a fallen tree. Shirley explained that Kenny had emotional problems and she was trying to help him. She said he was not happy with the way things were.

'I don't know what to do, I don't know if I should be here,' she said. 'Oh Jeremy, if only you were a bit older.'

I wished that conversation and walk hadn't taken place. My resolve of 'it's cool man' was now very much battered.

The affair started to fizzle out after that. We still all met up and then Shirley asked us to meet a new boyfriend she had. He was older than she and a doctor. Now we had invites there! I didn't particularly like this GP with Gingivitis, but she seemed happy and soon they were engaged. Micky and I went to the wedding. Kenny was, understandably, unavailable.

Kenny did have a fiery temper that rarely showed and then only when his privacy was threatened or when professionalism was compromised, as with Frankie

Howard. One summer's day Kenny was mowing the front lawn at Home Oaks when a man called out to him from the drive entrance gates.

'Hello Mr. Connor,' he said. 'Lovely day for mowing the lawn.'

The man leaned on the oak gates and Kenny waved at him and stopping the engine of the Suffolk Punch, he wandered over. He was used to this happening, it usually being for someone who wanted an autograph and a few words with the funny man. However, this man did not ask for an autograph. He did not produce pen and paper or a show programme. He just talked about how wonderful the house was and how lucky Kenny was.

'You must have earned a lot of money doing the *Carry On* films?' he suggested, turning his statement into a searching question at the end.

'I hope you enjoy them,' said Kenny politely but firmly.

'Oh yes, we all love them,' he replied. 'You do have a lovely house here, in such a secluded private road.'

'We like it,' said Kenny warily. 'You out walking?'

'Just thought I'd pop by,' he remarked. 'You love collecting antiques don't you? Read it in a magazine somewhere.'

'You don't want to believe everything you read in the press, you know,' Kenny chuckled and smiled in a dismissive sort of a way.

'I think it was in the *Evening Standard*. Quite a spread, a full feature,' he continued with purpose. 'Antiques are a good way of investing income at the moment, Mr. Connor. Much healthier than stocks and shares.'

'I must get on, and you need to keep walking,' Kenny said pointedly.

'Don`t be like that, Kenneth, I`m enjoying our conversation,' he said. 'Mind if I come in and have a look around?'

'No, you fucking can't! Now go!' he said angrily.

'No, it doesn`t work like that, Mr. Connor,' he said calmly.

'What are you talking about?!' asked Kenny. 'This is my property and you are not coming anywhere near it. Now be on your way or I'll call the police!'

'We're above the police, Mr. Connor. I`m here from the VAT, from Customs and Excise. I have the given right to enter a property at any time,' The VAT man smiled. 'I hope you understand now.'

'Are you now?' said Kenny. 'Wait here a minute'

Kenny walked off into the garden as the VAT man straightened up, expecting to enter the house. But he was wrong in his assumption. This was proved when Kenny returned dragging a spade.

'So you really want to come in then?' asked Kenny.

'Thank you, Mr. Connor. Yes,' said our friendly VAT man.

Kenny wielded the spade and smacked it down on the wooden gates.

'I`ll have your guts on this shovel before I let you in here!' he shouted angrily. 'Now fuck off before I make you!'

The VAT man took flight and headed off down the road with Kenny wielding the spade, loudly hurling abuse and making blood curdling noises. He chased him until the man was through the private road toll gate and then stood there as if on guard, watching him still running away. The toll gate keeper, Mr. Porter, casually come out of the keeper`s cottage in his bee keeper's outfit, in order to see what all the commotion was about.

'Are you alright, Mr. Connor?' he asked. 'Is that a burglar?'

'Worse,' said Kenny. 'The VAT man!'

'Ooh!' said Mr. Porter. 'I hope he doesn`t come after me.'

They stood there watching the VAT man until he had disappeared around the bend. The man never returned. No police or Customs officers came to arrest Kenny for attempted murder. Nothing happened! So, was this man a fraudster? A conman? Or was he simply a VAT man who had got it all wrong? Nothing ever transpired from this event.

One afternoon Kenny was at home having a kip by the log fire in the sitting room of Home Oaks. The doorbell rang and Micky went to answer it. There were two men standing in the porch and said they had come to do an interview with Kenneth Connor. Micky said she had been told nothing about this and that it was not in the diary. The reporters said that they had requested permission from Peter Rogers and that his office at Pinewood Studios had arranged it. Micky told them that they had better come in and take a seat in the hall while she went to tell Kenny. When she returned she offered them tea, saying that Mr. Connor would be with them shortly and went to the kitchen. Kenny emerged from the sitting room and after the usual greetings led them into the large oak panelled dining room with it sofas and scatter cushions. Kenny said he had been sleeping and was going to freshen up before being interviewed.

Kenny left the reporters and went straight upstairs to the equally large study that was directly above the dining room. Then he tried to listen to the reporters talking below. They were talking quietly and Kenny could only pick out odd words, but he deduced they were only talking about where to take photos and that they were 'lucky to get this'. Moving away to the other side of the study, and taking the phone on its long lead with him, Kenny rang the *Carry On* office and spoke to Audrey Skinner, Peter's long time PA. There had been no such arrangements for an interview. Kenny, now in a rage, stormed downstairs and confronted them.

'What the hell do you think you are playing at?' he demanded. 'You're both here under false pretences.'

'We are freelance journalists and we just want do a nice article on you,' they explained.

'Right, give me your names. I'm going to report you for this, it's illegal. It's trespass!' said Kenny fuming. 'Which paper are you doing this for?'

'We're doing it for ourselves,' they said. 'Then we'll see if we can sell it.'

'Well, you're bloody not! Names?!' demanded Kenny.

'Oh, don't be like that, Ken,' they said, trying to calm the situation. 'Anyway, we're here now.'

'Don't try and be so fucking casual about it! Get out of my house!' replied Kenny.

And with that he threw them out saying he was going to call the police. He watched them scurry away and jump in a car. Then he realised he had not got their names. Bugger! Number plate, get the number plate. Kenny grabbed his car keys, pulled on some shoes and took pursuit. They were only a few hundred yards up the road outside the school playing fields. Kenny jumped out of the car and ran over to them and tore open the driver's door, ripping the door strop away, so the door flapped around like a broken wing on a grounded bird. He demanded names again, but the door was grabbed out of his grasp and the car sped off with Kenny trying to read the number plate. Jumping back in the Jag, Kenny chased after them, but there was no sign of them at the top end of South Hill Avenue. Had they turned left up to Harrow Hill or right down to Sudbury? He decided to go to the South Harrow police station at the bottom of Roxeth Hill.

On his arrival at the police station, Kenny pulled into the car park at the side of the building and entered by the back door. While he was looking for a clue as to which way to go, Kenny noticed he had not done up his shoe laces. He was bending down to do them up when he heard voices coming from the door in front of him. It wasn't long before he realised that the voices belonged to the two journalists. The two men were saying they had been attacked by Kenneth Connor – and he was a maniac! Kenny then made his entrance through the door and came up behind the desk sergeant.

'I have come to report these two fakes for conning my wife into letting them into our house,' he declared angrily.

The sergeant spun round in his chair and came face-to-face with Kenny.

'What are you doing behind here Kenny, erm, Mr Connor?!' he asked. 'Get round the other side of the desk if you want to make a formal complaint!'

Kenny was ushered through the desk hatch to the other side. Meanwhile, the old sergeant told the reporters to shut up and stand still. He then spoke to them about trespass and false statements, the right procedures and police car parks. The journalists were then told that if they withdrew their complaint, there would be no further action against them. They agreed and he told them to leave while he dealt with Mr. Connor.

'Please don`t do that again, Kenny,' he begged. 'I know you are a celebrity, and do a lot of functions for us, but really!'

'It's so frustrating,' said Kenny sheepishly. 'I'm sorry, I'll be off now. Got to go to the theatre.'

Kenny then made for the hatch to exit the way he had come in.

'No you don't, Kenny,' said the sergeant. 'Go out the public entrance and round to the car park,' he continued. 'Oh! And Kenny, do up your shoe laces!'

Chapter Six

Farcing Around

After *Carry On Cleo*, Kenny didn't return to the *Carry On* series until the 1970 film, *Carry On Up the Jungle*. During the making of the latter, a behind-the-scenes documentary – *Carry On Forever* – was filmed at Pinewood. Kenny was asked to share his thoughts on the *Carry On* films for the programme:

> 'It's so professionally done. Everyone, right through, every facet – carpentry, props mechanics, electrics, everything. They know where they are, it's like a well-run ship. They're in, out, the job's done, and tons and tons of shots done during the day.'

He then went on to comment about the jungle set:

> 'It looks so realistic on the rushes you begin to wonder why people decide to go away to Ceylon on location to make a film when it can be done like this.'

Kenny missed the following film, *Carry On Loving*, but did join the cast of *Carry On Henry*, which was released in early 1971, in order to play the relatively small role of Lord Hampton of Wick.

In 1969, Thames TV signed many of the *Carry On* team up to the first-ever TV special, which was entitled *Carry On Christmas*. However, it wasn't until 1970 that Kenny first made an appearance in a *Carry On* TV spin-off. Entitled *Carry On Again Christmas*, Kenny played Doctor Dr. Livershake in a send-up of *Treasure Island*. Kenny appeared in a total of three Christmas specials for Thames. All of these were taped at their then studio base in Teddington, with the occasional bit of location filming thrown in for good measure. They were originally shown during Christmas 1970, 1972 and 1973. The 1972 and 1973 versions were both called *Carry On Christmas*, although the 1972 version had the subtitle of *Carry On Stuffing*. Incidentally, Kenny was later seen in clips featured in Thames' *Carry On Laughing* compilation series in 1981, and *Carry On Laughing's Christmas Classics* in 1983.

In the spring of 1971, the *Carry On* team found themselves without Kenny again for their next film, *Carry On Convenience*, due to other commitments. However, fans of Kenny's appearances in the *Carry On* films were able to see him appear on stage in the French farce, *Boeing Boeing*, that summer in the seaside town of Cliftonville, a suburb of Margate.

The plot of *Boeing Boeing* centres around two main characters. Bernard, which in this case played by MacDonald Hobley, a swinging bachelor architect living in an apartment in Paris, who has three stewardesses on the go, and timid, old friend. Robert. Kenny played the latter. New, faster Boeing airliners eventuate all three girlfriends arriving at the same time, and Robert ends up having to cover for Bernard by making excuses and hiding all of the stewardesses from each other.

All the cast enjoyed this Brian Rix-style bed-hopping with stewardesses popping in and out of doorways and cupboards, and Kenny`s Robert becoming more and more frantic. Great fun. The theatre, not. It wasn't a real theatre, it was a converted commercial laundry with painted egg boxes on the walls for sound baffling! Up around this had grown a full blown fun fair with night club.

Kenny dreaded the thought of having to spend months in a bed and breakfast or a tacky tourist hotel, so he brought his boat, the John Francis, downstream from the Upper Thames through London and up the River Medway to The Medway Bridge Marina. From there it was a fifty-mile fast road trip to the theatre, and this suited him just fine to get the separation, but still enjoy doing the show.

Kenny became firm and lifelong friends with the company manager, Robert Corp-Reader, whose father was Ralph Reader, the creator of *The Gang Show*. When Bob`s wife, who worked in TV, became ill with cancer, Bob had to come off the road to be with her at their home in Bourne End, Bucks. This is where the Marina is that the John Francis was moored at. Now, Kenny had invested in the Marina and knew that the owner and his friend, Tom Jones, was needing a hand in this expanding project. So he put Bob up for it and he became general manager.

Kenny and Bob would meet up most weekends in the club bar telling showbiz tales and swapping terrible jokes. Micky always insisted on cooking a full roast in the small oven on board, and those lunchtime drinking sessions would often run on. Inevitably, Micky used to get annoyed at having to hold back the lunch, and I used to be sent to get him out of the club.

'Fancy a half, Jeremy?' Bob would ask.

Then we`d all be in the shit!

One day, Kenny came back to the boat a little worse for wear. He announced that he was going to take a walk around the deck just to do a check. Now, the fore deck hatch used to be removed to let out the heat when Micky was cooking. We were serving up in the galley when these legs come flying through the hatch, bounced on the bunk and shot back up! Micky and I were in hysterics. Kenny came inside with blood starting to pour down his shin, acting as though nothing had happened.

'By ya stupid bugger, Ken!' she Micky, still laughing.

One night, near Margate, Kenny came to a police road block on the Thanet Way while driving back to the boat. The police waved him down with torches and he lowered his window. One of the torches was then shone directly into his face.

'Bloody hell! It's Kenneth Connor!' exclaimed one of the policemen.

The same policeman explained to Kenny that the road block was due to illegal Indian immigrants being dropped off nearby by small boats. They revealed that the immigrants were then driven in vehicles up to London. Police note books were then thrust through the window for autographs before Kenny was allowed on his way. He just wanted to get back on the road to his beloved boat and his bacon and eggs and port!

Thinking about the Thanet Way reminds me that towards the end of the season, Kenny had his only ever road accident. He drove straight into the back of a slow moving car that had come out of a country lane, knocking it into a third car. He hadn't seen the car pull out of the side road, as he had been trying to find a station on the radio. The police turned up, as someone from a nearby cottage had heard the noise of the crash and rang them. It was the police who then radioed for an ambulance and tow trucks. No one was seriously injured, although I think someone put a claim against Kenny for whiplash. Two of the cars had to be towed, but the Jag was still drivable, so he took it easy into the theatre. He then rang the AA from the stage door to organise a hire car and trailer to a take it to a body shop in London. This accident shook him up big time and he never bought a fast car again. Kenny sold the car shortly after it was repaired and bought a Morris 1300 Countryman.

I said that Kenny only had one car accident, but in 1955 he got a small part as a taxi driver in the classic Ealing comedy film, *The Lady Killers*. The part called for him to drive the taxi into a railway station. On the first take he swung the taxi into the station, hitting a high curb with a front wheel, snapping the axle in the process. He was certainly no stunt driver!

When the summer holidays started, I caught a train down to Margate. I took a cab to Cliftonville and walked through the funfair where I found the stage door. The place was a shabby affair with pokey little dressing rooms. A place of no character. I dumped my bag and wrote a message on the mirror in grease paint saying I was here and at the funfair. Funfairs are funfairs and you end up spending more than you bargained for. My Saturday morning job money was depleting rapidly. More importantly, I was starving.

I went back to the theatre, for want of a better expression, where by now Kenny had finished the show, taken off his make-up and changed. We hugged and off we went.

'We're going to a right dive bar for a drink and then back to the boat to eat. Bacon and eggs?'

'Great, I'm starving,' I replied. 'Got any tomatoes for frying?'

He gripped me in his deadly headlock.

'Don't be poncey! Come on,' he snapped.

Kenny pulled the brim of his skipper's hat down over his eyes and we burst out of the stage door to some startled autograph hunters who shuffled backwards out of the way.

'Shut up you!' he said, impersonating a policeman. 'I'm taking you straight round to the police station.'

We bundled on and faded into the fairground crowd.

'That fooled them!' said Kenny laughing.

We then disappeared down the stairs into the dive bar.

Kenny was very loyal to his supporters. He would always stop in the street to sign autographs, pose for photographs and to chat. Micky and I would be hanging around in the background waiting. But to him the stage door was different and work was work. It was his psyche. To him the other side of the stage door was his work place, a place to prepare and compose for the job ahead. Therefore a private place of space. And when the job was done, and every energy expended, he wanted to do what everyone else does at the end of the day – get the hell out of his workplace! As I mentioned, Kenny would speak to everyone in the street, but if ever there were fans hanging around outside his property, he would chase them off very rudely.

Anyway, back to the dive bar. This was no dive bar – it was a disco! To a fifteen-year-old it was a discovery. The lighting and the wall of sound blew me away! I just wish I could remember what sort of sounds they played. There was a side bar where you could get away from the noise and that was where I met Bob Reader for the first time. I immediately warmed to him. Kenny decided to order a round.

'Three pints of muck please.'

'Bitter or mild muck?' the barmaid replied.

'Oh the bitter, your best muck,' he said.

I thought that this must be some kind of private joke they had going on.

'Why do you call it muck? I asked.

'Just wait until you taste it,' said Bob.

God knows what it was, but it was the most insipid stuff. It sort of tasted like beer, but had no body or strength. You could drink muck all night and still pass a breathalyser.

It turned out the dive bar was a nightclub called Haydes. The club was a new edition to the complex and the cast of *Boeing Boeing* had all been invited to the official opening night. As you can imagine, I was keen to get an invite, but realised I was going to have to work on the old man if I was going to be in with a chance of attending.

We soon said our goodbyes and went to get the car. Kenny had bought one of the first Jaguar XJ6s off the production line. With 4.2 litres of cruising power we were soon back at the boat. It was great to be back on board the John Francis and with bacon and eggs and a port consumed, we bunked down for the night.

Kenny`s bacon and eggs were something special. So, just in case you want the recipe, here it is:

The bacon has to be fried at some speed. First you cut off the rind and reserve to chew raw while cooking. Checking for when the bacon is ready requires a certain test. Hold a knife between thumb and forefinger at the back end of the hilt, allowing the blade to drop on the bacon. If it bounces up off the bacon, it's not quite ready. If, when you drop the knife and the bacon cracks, it's done. Whip it out quick! Perfect! The fried egg has to be just right. It must be burnt black all around the edge of the white, while ensuring that the yolk retains a reasonable amount of the uncooked opaque membrane mucus on the top. Just right! Serve with chunks of bread with too much butter on and salt. Kenny`s bacon and eggs. Done!

And here's the recommended accompanying drink:

A very milky instant coffee with some still undissolved granules floating on top.

Kenny said he couldn't cook because the British army ruined his taste buds. I think he was being too modest, don't you?

I soon fell in line with Kenny's daily routine between boat and theatre. Every day he had to suffer an ordeal as he walked through the fun fair to the laundry. You had to pass by a bingo stall. And every day the bingo caller would stop calling the numbers mid-game to speak over his microphone to his players.

'Ladies and gentlemen,' he'd start by saying. 'If you turn around now you will see the *Carry On* star Kenneth Connor on his way to work. Yeah folks, Kenneth Connor is actually appearing LIVE on stage!!'

Kenny would just smile, but more than once I heard him mutter, 'Of course I'm live on stage, you fucking twat!'

Kenny had to find things to do for his teenage son, and we would drive out to the beaches and skim stones, bomb driftwood and go to the mussel and cockle sheds for the freshest cockles you could ever taste. We'd go into Ramsgate and hang around the inner harbour, watching the fishermen, whilst eating prawn cocktails and drinking Guinness. We drove through the countryside, passing orchards and hop gardens nearly ready to harvest. The Garden of England spread out before us. It made you proud to be British. We both decided we loved Kent and the English summer was worth much more than Ibiza!

I noticed that Kenny was getting tired and he still had one month to go. Thanks to me, he had been missing out on his pre-show nap and I told him to ease up. A guy who worked on the marina lent us an old speedboat that belonged to the yard. They used it for patrolling up and down daily to check the moorings and the security of the boats. There was a lot of money tied up there, in more ways than one. So, while Kenny had a well-deserved afternoon rest, I would fuel up the outboard tank with two stroke and tear up and down the River Medway with the cold spray pummelling my face.

When matinee day came around, I decided I really didn't want to hang around in Cliftonville for the afternoon and evening, so I opted to stay on board and clean the boat and have the late night supper ready. We went and got some provisions and then Kenny went off to do two performances. It turned out that he had been surviving off of nothing but bacon and eggs for two months and the grease around the galley proved it. I said I'd do something more healthy, and first I decided to have a clean-up in the boat. You might think it odd that a fifteen-year-old would offer to clean anything, but I loved that boat as much as Kenny. It was a welcoming haven for us. It was my playmate, my brother, my sister.

Kenny commissioned the boat to be built by the master boat builder, Tom Jones, in 1968. It was completed in the summer of 1969. It was the year that men landed on the moon and Kenny landed on the Thames! Tom had built three other thirty-foot off-shore cruisers. The cockpits, or helms, were all situated mid-vessel and all open to the air, with hooding on metal frames to pull up into place for weather protection. Kenny did not want 'pram hoods'. They don't last long in the English weather and soon look tatty. Kenny and Micky wanted a proper covered wheelhouse.

The boat was to become Kenny's biggest financial commitment, apart from Home Oaks, and his biggest project outside of acting. That's probably why he got so focused on it. He sat down with Micky and drew rough plans for the wheelhouse before taking them to the building yard on the Thames, just below Windsor Castle. He handed them to Tom for the engineer's plans to be drawn up. Tom was uncertain about adding so much weight to the vessel. He was also concerned about stability in a sea condition and how it would look physically to the eye. All the same, Kenny demanded more. All of the boats that Tom built had gleaming white hulls and Kenny wanted a navy blue hull.

After many meetings and lots of pouring over the plans and calculations, Kenny's aim was finally achieved and full construction started. The hull was made of fibreglass and the superstructure was crafted out of teak, mahogany and pine. While the boat was powered by twin Mercedes diesels. Now if it was not a master piece I would stop here, but here's what it actually looked like:

The dark blue hull had white decks and cabin roofs. The sides were of highly varnished teak. The wheelhouse had sliding doors and a slide back roof hatch to let the sun in. Everything inside was wood. Starting from the bow, there was a cabin with two bunks and a covered wash basin. In between this and the main living area or saloon, was to one side the bathroom, or heads, and to the other a wet weather gear cupboard. In the saloon, there was a full galley to one side, and dining area to the other. All the upholstery was of plush, but hard wearing Draylon of an aqua marine colour. Going upstairs led to the wheel house, the floor of which was all hatches trimmed with brass. These gave access to the engine room. The steering position had a huge array of dials like an aircraft! Then down more steps into the stern cabin to another two bunks and washing facilities. There were davits on the transom and a small sailing dinghy with matching blue hull and flag poles on the stern and main cabin roofs.

Kenny named the John Francis after his father. It was his memorial to him. Ah! Hence the blue hull, Kenny had been building a small royal yacht – a Britannia – because his father had, of course, served on a royal yacht!

Kenny was late back from work. Where the hell was he? It had gone very cold. I'd put the oven on to get some warmth and laid out our late night feast. Then I heard footsteps on the floating pontoon and he bounded in full of excitement.

'Hello,' he said. 'Have I got a tale for you!'

Kenny then went into the forward cabin and, pulling the carpet up, he removed the hatch cover that gave access to the bilge and grabbed a couple of Long Life beers (anyone else remember that stuff?). That below waterline area made a good chilly bin. Not even noticing the spread of food, he pulled open the cans and lit up a cigarette. He was fighting back tears of laughter as he told me, and I was soon in tears too. Kenny told me that the police road block had returned to the Thanet Way. The torches appeared up ahead, waving him to slow down. He braked hard and slowed to a crawl turning off all the lights. The torches started wavering in an erratic manner and he stopped short of the block so the police had to walk down the road to him. He looked down and away from the driver's window as a torch was shone in.

'Wind down the window,' said a copper.

'There's no-one in here but me,' replied Kenny in an Indian accent.

Now there were torches pointing in from all round the car.

'Wind down the window!' a policeman demanded angrily.

Kenny lowered the window, pulled back his hat and beamed a big smile at them.

'You bastard, Mr. Connor!' said a shocked voice.

All of the policemen started roaring with laughter, their dull night being livened up. But our boys in blue were annoyed they had not recognised the car and its personal number plate.

'Don't tell our superiors, Kenny!' they begged.

With the tale told, and another couple of beers out, we tucked into our supper. Micky always left Kenny a tray of food when he was working in the West End, so I had copied that. I prepared slices of cold ham and wedges of brie. There were pickles and beetroot and coleslaw with French bread and butter. To round it all off, the star on the plate was tinned Heinz vegetable salad. Great!

The following week was the formal opening of the nightclub and I'd managed to persuade Kenny to let me go. It was a mid-week private do, with local dignitary and traders being invited, so it wasn't going to be late

The cast all wandered down to Haydes after the show. The place was full of full of mayoral and commerce chains of office, not exactly disco-goers. I had fun, though, dancing with the lovely ASM understudies! Kenny was getting his ear bent by the mayor, but Bob rescued him and they went to the side bar. There was a significant buffet laid out that was hardly touched until we arrived. Now, if you have never catered for actors before, you'll know that they're the Gannets of the arts world!

The buffet consumed, dancing resumed. At midnight Kenny caught my attention. It was time to go. He`d had enough, and I wasn`t going to push my luck. We walked back to the Jag and suggested that I'd better drive. Kenny had been teaching me to drive since I was nine, driving up and down the private, gated roads where we lived. The cars had all been Jags or the fabulous Daimler V8, but I'd never driven this particular model before. Off we went in the dark and all was going well. He told me to slow up as I screeched around a roundabout. I looked at the dials and I was only doing thirty mph. Oh shit! No I wasn`t, I was looking at the rev counter. The speedo said seventy-five mph! We were nearly back when I rounded a bend and there was a Police Slow sign. We pulled over and swapped seats quickly and drove on. There was no road block, just the forgotten sign. We got back to the boat and had a drink, both pondering what the penalty would be for allowing a fifteen-year-old drive on the open road!

I left by train the following week to go home and catch up with friends and prepare for the next school term. Kenny rang Micky from the theatre the next week to say the producers had come to see the show and to take the cast to dinner. Over a good nosh they offered Kenny summer season in Torquay the next year. If he was going to do it, he would take the John Francis.

'Count me in, dad,' I enthused.

It was time for Kenny to return to the *Carry On* series again, and this time it was to play British Rail employee, Mr. Tidey, in *Carry On Matron*. The majority of the film, which was released in May 1972, was based in a maternity hospital, and Kenny's character spent all of his time waiting for his wife – played by Joan Sims – to give birth! At one point, his frustration resulted in him calling for matron to give his wife 'dynamite!' in an attempt to induce the birth of their child! And although matron doesn't oblige, a gang of crooks, led by Sid Carter (played by Sid James), does!

Kenny also began playing roles in the Arthur Lowe radio sitcom, *Parsley Sidings*, back in 1971. In many ways, it was the forerunner to the David Croft and Richard Spendlove TV sitcom, *Oh, Doctor Beeching!* At the time, Kenny told the *Radio Times*:

'I love radio. You have a silent giggle with the studio audience. It's a purely mental world, which you wouldn't want to see translated into visual terms.'

Prolific writer, Jim Eldridge, who worked on *Parsley Sidings*, still has great memories of working on the sitcom:

'*Parsley Sidings*, which was my first sitcom, centred around a very small railway station somewhere in the Midlands, and starred Arthur Lowe as the station master, Horace Hepplewhite, Ian Lavender as his son, Bert, Liz Fraser as station announcer, Gloria Simpkins, and Kenneth Connor as the dubious spiv-like porter, Percy Valentine, and also the extremely ancient, bronchitically wheezing, hard-of-hearing signalman, Bradshaw. The series was produced by Edward Taylor and ran for two series (twenty-one episodes) between 1971 and 1973. Since then, I have gone onto create fifteen series for BBC & ITV in the UK, and had two hundred and fifty radio scripts and two hundred and fifty TV scripts broadcast... but it all started with *Parsley Sidings*.

'Ken was an absolute delight to work with. Not only was he a comedy genius – his timing and delivery were the absolute best – but he was one of the nicest people I ever worked with in my forty plus years as a scriptwriter. Watching him work a live audience (all the episodes were recorded in front of an audience) and making the script so much funnier because of the way he handled the lines, was an education for me in how to write comedy.

'Once I saw how brilliant Ken was at handling more than one character, and how much comedy he could get out of everything, I was eager to write more eccentric characters for Ken for the show. The result was that Ken – as well as playing Percy Valentine and Bradshaw – also played starring 'guest roles': a very precious actor on location at the station for a film, the shifty Head of MI5, a bumbling bureaucrat – and many, many more. But for me my favourite 'other character' (and also, I know this was Ken's favourite – because he said so on a Radio programme about his career) was Clara, the station hen.

'It began when I wrote a scene between Arthur Lowe, as the unhappy station master in conversation with Clara the station hen, telling his sadness about his son's lack of abilities, and expressing his worry about his son's future. With just the one word "Bk", Ken as Clara, was sympathetic ("Bk"), indignant (Bk bk!") frantic ("bk bk bk bk bk!!") and he ran the whole gamut of emotions as he and Arthur had this serious meaningful conversation. Arthur and Ken were brilliant in this scene, the way they played off each other. The studio audience were in hysterics at them as they did this scene as straight drama, which made it even funnier.

'After that, whenever I could, I would write a scene for Clara the hen for Ken – and he was always brilliant. Never was a chicken played with such a range of easily understandable emotions with just "bk". Ken Connor, the comedy genius, and someone to whom I will always be grateful for teaching me about comedy.'

Ian Lavender also remembers the happy period he spent working with Kenny on *Parsley Sidings*:

'Apart from his role as the porter, Ken was also Clara the hen. And with only one word or cluck as a script, he invented a whole chicken life not only through his clucked conversations, but with his physical interpretation of the part too – on radio! The audiences would laugh at what they saw, not heard, and in a sound medium too. Arthur Lowe would act miffed about it, complaining that the audiences at home would never understand what was going on, but then turn away and giggle uncontrollably at Ken's Clara!

'Ken knew exactly what he was doing and made the studio audience forget what a false situation they were in. He then ensured that they were in the right mood for the rest of the dialogue.

'I always thought that Parsley Sidings had it in itself to be a rather delightful TV programme and I know that it was mooted at one point. But who knows for what reason it didn't go any further at the time. Arthur Lowe died and it became one of the vast number of delightful might-have-beens in the history of entertainment.'

The following year, 1972, saw the *Carry On* team head for the Mediterranean island of Els Bels – well, Pinewood Studios – for the making of *Carry On Abroad*. The cast was filled with a huge number of series favourites. They included Sid James, Kenneth Williams, Joan Sims, Peter Butterworth, Hattie Jacques, Bernard Bresslaw, Barbara Windsor and June Whitfield. Veteran team member Charles Hawtrey also returned for what was to be his last *Carry On* film.

During a spot of location work for *Abroad*, the cast and crew were filming on a coach in Slough. As Kenny, who was playing Stanley Blunt, boarded the coach with his on-screen wife, played by June Whitfield, he turned to Sid and Joan and spoke quite confidentially.

'You wouldn't happen to have some spare bromide would you?' he asked politely. 'You see, the jogging of the coach excites my wife!'

As you can imagine, this left the cast on the coach in hysterics!

Another scene in the film was far less funny for Kenny and June to shoot. You may recall that in one scene the character of Stanley had to jump onto his wife, Evelyn, in bed, fired up by a need for passion. Well, on landing on the bed, the floor immediately gave way and they fell through the hole – bed and all! But although Kenny managed to successfully keep his full body on the bed, he did injure his back to the point whereby he had to take three days off from the filming to recover.

Chapter Seven

Friends And Enemies

The summer of 1972 saw Kenny join Charles Hawtrey and Bernard Bresslaw on stage the for the summer season in Torquay. Written by Sam Cree, in typical *Carry On* style, *Stop It Nurse* ran twice-nightly on Monday to Saturday for the season. Barry Howard, who went on to achieve great success playing Barry Stuart-Hargreaves in *Hi-de-Hi!*, also appeared in the production.

It was arranged for the John Francis to be taken by road on a low loader down to Devon, and was placed on a mooring in the outer harbour on Princess Pier, Torquay. The rehearsals took place in London with the final week in the theatre, which was on a pier on the inner harbour.

I travelled down to join Kenny in the June after my exams were finished. By the time I arrived the boat had been moved to a buoy in the middle of the outer harbour as the Princess Pier was not suitable. Every night it was full of noisy youths and the weekends were worse as the boats got pelted with beer and pop bottles. Ah, the joy of tourists, or 'grockles', as the Devonians call them! Bob, the show's stage manager, had his own feelings about grockles.

'I don't call them grockles,' he said. 'I call them haemorrhoids because they come down in bunches, go red and they're a pain in the arse!'

The mooring in the middle of the harbour was out of harm's way and silent, but it was made it more difficult to get ashore with the dinghy having to be used. No pontoon walkway out there. Kenny had a word with Bob, who was also a trawler man, and he arranged for the dinghy to be stored in one of the store sheds on the harbour. So poor Kenny had been rowing ashore every night before dragging the dinghy up the concrete launch ramp and storing it away in the shed. He then repeated the journey at the end of each day.

'Glad you're here son,' he said on my arrival. 'I've had it with the rowing. We can use the outboard now there's two of us.'

With that, two months of fun and adventure began and what a time we had. The show churned on and on and was relentless. As the curtain fell on the first house and the actors walked off stage, the deputy stage manager was already giving fifteen minutes warning to the cast for the next performance! The stage was quickly reset, the front of house staff changed the audiences at record speed, and then off they went again!

The nearest watering hole to the theatre was the Marine Tavern. It was an absolute dive (yes, another 'dive'!), but most of the cast used it before the first show. We all sat at the bar drinking our beer. Well, that was all except Charles Hawtrey, who sat at a low table with his personal manager, Tony. There was always a bottle of Moet on the table, which Charles called his lemonade. Tony was very close to Hawtrey and looked after him well.

Sometimes when the first show was on, Tony and I would go out in his little Triumph Herald to explore all the lovely old villages around Torbay. He loved the countryside and the sea, so it's no wonder they moved to the seaside town of Deal together.

One day, Bob quizzed Kenny as to how much fishing we were doing on the boat. And when Kenny said 'none,' he said he would make up some mackerel lines. He did this backstage during one of the performances. They were long lines with nine feathered hooks on, all spaced out. These were then wound on to a wooden frame loom. Kenny was really pleased and thanked Bob profusely. He told us to fish around Ore Stone Rock (apparently gold had been found there).

The next good day, we cruised out and fished for five hours. We caught one Mackerel! We headed back and cooked it as instructed. Gutted – in more ways than one – we put it in a baking tray with cider and a bay leaf and stuck it in the oven. By the time it was cooked there was about three inches of fish each. We motored ashore in the dinghy to find a café. The café we found was great and run by two gay guys who did great home cooking. Even now, I can remember that their fresh tomato and parsley soup was to die for! All done, we headed off to the theatre.

We now had no access to the net store to stow the dinghy as the shed was getting very busy. Kenny bought a chain and padlock and we would secure the dinghy to one of the iron rings set into the boat ramp. We had started using a restaurant very nearby called The Hansom Cab and the owner let us store the oars and outboard in the entrance lobby. Now the Hansom Cab was a fun eating house run by an ex-entertainer. It was decked out in a Victorian style with menu to match. There was a Pianola situated in the corner, which the owner would sing along to and play the trumpet while being dressed in old music hall costume. Kenny loved the menu: bangers and bubble and squeak, steak and kidney and meat pie and liquor. Then there was lemon syllabub and sherry trifle. We had to go back there every night to get the dinghy equipment and so it became a regular haunt. The comedian, Peter Goodwright, started coming as well. He was working in a variety show at the Princess Theatre and we would sit in the bar and he would tell his shaggy dog stories.

They were hysterical and none had an ending. He used to say, 'The ending is up to you'.

It was becoming quite a task to walk round the inner harbour's three sides as it was now peak season, and it was crowded with hobbling pensioners and dawdling tourists. Kenny named the three sides Hernia Way, Pile Passage and Haemorrhoidal Walk. We would speed walk through the masses in that ludicrous fashion that you see on the Olympics overtaking people like you were on a Formula One track.

The promenades had other hazards. One morning we were walking along the main prom towards the Princess Theatre when we saw a large Yorkshire man waddling towards us with camera resting on his large beer belly.

'Hey up, Kenneth,' he said cheerily. 'Saw your show last night.'

'Oh, good,' replied Kenny.

'It was shit!' said the Yorkshire man.

'Fuck off,' snapped Kenny.

'I don't believe Kenneth Connor just said that to me,' said the man to his equally large wife.

Kenny stormed off and I followed behind him grinning.

We had arranged for my best friend to come and join us on board for a few weeks. So, Michael Popper joined the crew of the John Francis, and what fun we had. Mike and I had been at the same prep school from the age of six. Starting off as day boys, we both became boarders and the school was only three doors away from Home Oaks! Anyway, Mike's parents split up and divorced when he was twelve, and he started staying weekends at Home Oaks. Mike decided to adopt Kenny as a father. Kenny loved him, as he did all the younger generation – the eternal teenager, that's what he wanted to be.

With Mike on board joining in the routine of the day, we all had an enjoyable balance. Well, apart from Kenny teasing Mike who has always had bad eyesight and wore huge specs.

'Just as well you are Jewish,' Kenny used to say, as he tucked him up into his bunk each night. 'You need a nose like that to support those specs.'

'You can talk, Mr. Connor!' Mike used to reply.

Kenny had to wear specs from the age of seven and, as all his fans will know, had a prominent nose!

We had enjoyed good weather on land and sea, but then it turned foul, and I mean dangerous, on the water. But never one to turn his back on an adventure, Kenny decided to give the John Francis a sea trial in heavy weather. We had prepared to set sail by storing everything away and packing the crockery draws with cushions and sleeping bags. With the engines warmed up, and the dinghy tied to our mooring buoy, we cast off and headed out. You could see the waves passing the harbour wall and the tops of them were above the height of those walls. They must have been twelve foot or more and the black flag was flying which meant even the ferries could not operate! We were up to full throttle as we powered out of the harbour entrance and turned hard to port to face the oncoming waves, which we climbed, and on hitting the top of each wave, Kenny would throttle back and we'd surf down the other side into the trough between the waves then throttle back up for the next ascent. It was soon obvious that we'd bitten off more than we could chew. Kenny's face went very serious and his mouth tight lipped.

'What's wrong?' I asked.

'I'm trying to work out how to turn around without capsizing,' he replied nervously.

Holy shit, I thought!

103

For the next ten minutes we timed the distance between the waves and the time in the trough and he decided to turn in the trough which was out of the wind. It was eerie in the troughs with no sound of the wind and you could hear the echo of the engines coming back off the sides of the waves.

'Okay, here we go', said Kenny.

When we plunged down the next wave into the trough, he then put on full throttle and spun the helm to hard starboard. We were now side on and the next wave approaching. Kenny wrenched the starboard throttle into reverse to speed us round, and she came around just in time and he put both throttles full ahead.

It was easier on the way back. And as we got level with the harbour wall, he turned to starboard again in the trough. We belted in, narrowly missing the breakwater, tied up and checked the boat for damage. Then we sat in silence with beers, the adrenaline receding.

The sea was still high the next day. Mike and I decided to take the dinghy out with its tiny outboard and give it a go. We had gone out early leaving Kenny asleep. Mike was in the bow and I on the outboard arm. We made it down into the first trough okay and started to climb up the next wave, the one and a half horse power engine echoing back at us in the hollow. Mike had got a soaking being in the bow and had moved onto the centre seat. The problem was that on reaching the top of the wave the wind got under the now light bow and started to flip us like a backward somersault.

'Get back in the bow, Mike, quick!' I shouted.

Mike threw himself forward and the bow came down. I spun the small boat round in the next trough and went straight back. We didn't tell Kenny about our near disaster for a few years!

Kenny had a new late night favourite meal and he called it 'Spaceman's Breakfast'. The Apollo astronauts had a breakfast tradition before blasting off consisting of steak, fried egg and chips. So, out would come the chip pan, which was a bit of a dodgy thing on a rocking boat, but it had to be done. We would have this nearly every other night, and Mike loved it. He loved food with the Connors and would often turn up at Home Oaks in the weekend as he knew there would be bacon sandwiches around. His mother was very kosher, so he had absolutely no chance of a bacon sarnie back at home!

One of Kenny's fellow cast members from *Stop it Nurse*, Anita Graham, was kind enough to jot down the following musings on Kenny and of the actual production:

'I have very fond memories of *Stop It Nurse* and working with Kenneth. It was only my second or third job, and I played Nurse Gloria, in a very short skirt, while Kenneth was a patient. The production was a bit like a *Carry On* film brought to life on stage!

'Kenneth was incredibly popular. He was a very private, kind, gentle and reflective man off-stage. But, in my opinion, he was like a lot of actors who became household names for their comedy work, he was an underused actor

'I also worked with Kenneth some years later in a John Chapman and Jeremy Lloyd farce, set in a fall-out shelter during the threat of World War Three, called *Keeping Down With the Joneses*. Kenneth played an Indian milkman – something that would cause outrage these days – brilliantly. He was a very funny man.

'Anyway, back to *Stop It Nurse*. It was great fun, but I don't think we socialised much. In fact, the three *Carry On* stars – Kenneth, Bernard and Charles – in the show seemed to lead very separate lives. They were three very different people. It was a long, twice-nightly season staged back in the days when more people holidayed in British seaside towns. The audiences loved it. Every performance was different, and it was difficult keeping a straight face most nights! It was a lovely feeling being on stage making people laugh!

'I was very lucky to work with Kenneth.'

At the end of August, Mike had to head home so it was just Kenny and me again. All the same, we had more adventures on the water.

There was a policeman who would come backstage when on patrol to have a mug of tea and watch a bit of the show from the wings. He got chatting with Kenny and when he heard that we were living on the water, he invited us out to join him with his fishing club. Constable Dennis Smith would pick us up from the boat ramp at four-thirty am on a Sunday and drive us to Brixham to pick up the boat. The boat that the club chartered was an old wooden trawler called 'The Bread Winner'. It came with a skipper and mate whose accents were so thick West Country, it was hard to understand them. We went 'wreck' fishing, travelling out to sea for about an hour or two to the location of the wreck. They would locate it exactly using a depth sounder that printed out the sea bed and there you could see the shape of the wreck. The crew put out a sea anchor and we would drift over the sunken vessel and pull out massive conger eels, which would fight you hard.

Kenny caught the largest ling of the summer and was eventually presented with a trophy. On the return, we all gutted and cut the congers into steaks placing them in plastic dustbins. There was so much that most of the catch was distributed around the old people's homes.

Some Sunday evenings, Kenny and I would go and watch rock and pop bands. The theatre was turned into a gig hall most Sunday nights, and we would stand at the back of the stalls and watch the likes of David Bowie, The Electric Light Orchestra and Wishbone Ash.

All in all, it was an amazing summer!

Towards the end of the run of *Stop It Nurse*, Kenny was approached by Cyril Fletcher and his wife, the cabaret artiste, Betty Astell, to do panto. Kenny said yes and quickly asked if there could be a part in it for yours truly! Cyril and Betty had their own production company that staged pantos every year in Cheltenham and Cambridge. Cyril would direct and appear in one, while Betty did the other.

A few days later, there was a letter at the stage door for Kenny. It was from the Fletchers, asking us both to attend a meeting at the Metropolitan Hotel, Torquay. We duly did as they asked, and the deal was done. We were both asked to do *Cinderella* at Cheltenham, with Kenny playing Buttons, and me one of the Broker's Men. We were both ecstatic, and all this just before I was about to return to London. I had to get some singing lessons fast! Kenny and I made a night of it at The Hansom Cab and then it was time to move on. The John Francis was brought back and Kenny stayed in a hotel for the last week.

In 1973, Kenny played Mayor Frederick Bumble in *Carry On Girls*, which was set around a beauty contest called Miss Fircombe. Although two *Carry On* films had been made each year since the series had started back in 1958, *Carry On Girls* was the only film to be made that year. This was to start a precedent, as only one *Carry On* film, including the compilation film, *That's Carry On!*, would then be made every year until the main series ground to a halt in 1978, after the release of *Carry On Emmannuelle*.

As with *Abroad* the previous year, the cast list for *Girls* was a strong one, despite the absence of Kenneth Williams, Charles Hawtrey and Hattie Jacques. Present, however, were the likes of Sid James, Barbara Windsor, Joan Sims, Bernard Bresslaw, June Whitfield, Peter Butterworth, Jack Douglas, Patsy Rowlands, (who played Kenny's wife, Mildred Bumble) and Jimmy Logan.

Going all out for laughs, writer Talbot Rothwell penned a bikini-clad fight scene, which took place in the reception area and lounge of the hotel belonging to Connie Philpotts (Joan Sims), the love interest of Sidney Fiddler (Sid James). It proved to be one of the biggest highlights of the film, and was not the only scene in which poor Kenny had to lose his trousers in the name of comedy!

Other highlights of the film include the scene in which Kenny, as Frederick Bumble, is seen playing with a toy boat in the bath. That is until Augusta Prodworthy (June Whitfield) decides to march into the bathroom, with her photographer son, Larry (Robin Askwith), for a row.

The troubled marriage of Frederick and Mildred Bumble finally reaches its climax in the Pier Theatre. Mildred, seizing her chance to rebel against her husband, sends Frederick crashing under the stage via a trap door while he's attempting to give a speech to a drenched and disappointed audience.

Away from the *Carry On* team, Kenny's busy 1973 also saw him take part in an international tour with the comedy play, *My Fat Friend*. Charles Laurence's brilliant comedy, which originally opened in 1972 at the Theatre Royal, Brighton, with Kenneth Williams and Jennie Linden in the cast, features a young woman who goes on a diet and takes exercise in order to attract a member of the opposite sex.

The cast members of Connor's tour were Dilys Watling, Christopher Matthews and Jonathan Burn. The play toured several venues in South Africa before finally returning to tour the UK. I auditioned for the role that Christopher subsequently played, but the producer, Jan Butlin, quite-rightly, thought I looked too young. So instead I went to Torquay to work on *Busman's Holiday* with some of the cast members of *On the Buses*. It was probably as well, as the tour of South Africa was more than a little eventful!

I have added the following three newspaper reports because I think they give an insightful account into what Kenny went through during this part of the tour. The first report is from an edition of the *Sunday Express*, which was published on Sunday 22 July 1973:

'FAT FRIEND' TWO NO LONGER FRIENDS.

A personal feud between two top British actors became public at the Johannesburg Civic Theatre last week when comedian Kenneth Connor, star of *My Fat Friend*, allegedly told fellow actor Jonathan Burn to "shut up" while they were on stage.

Mr Burn, 33, star of the London musical *Oh! Calcutta!*, in which he appeared nude before one million people, this week asked for a court order to be issued against Mr. Connor.

The order, which is expected to be served in Durban tomorrow, where the play will run until August 4, seeks to restrain Mr. Connor from threatening Mr. Burn with violence or directing abusive language at him.

The two actors have been at loggerheads since *My Fat Friend* opened in Johannesburg four weeks ago.

The dispute came to a head last Saturday night when Mr. Connor, veteran of more than twenty *Carry On* films (should be seventeen!), allegedly directed a personal remark, clearly audible, at Mr. Burn.

It allegedly happened during the second scene – and before a capacity audience.

Mr. Connor was alleged to have said: "Oh, why doesn`t he (Mr. Burn) shut up?"

The claimed statement was said in the presence of Mr. Burn, who plays the role of the boyfriend of Dilys Watling, the "fat girl", and Christopher Matthews, the young Scotsman.

Mr. Connor, I was told, appears to have made the remark because of two unscripted interjections by Mr. Burn.

The interjections consisted of "Ummmm" and "Oh" while Mr. Connor was speaking.

Mr. Burn, I was told, had interjected before believing they were artistically correct, and Mr. Connor had not lodged any complaint.

The young British actor appeared disturbed at the alleged remark.

He was concerned over the incident, and asked to see Mr. Connor outside his dressing room after the show.

Another row developed and Mr. Connor allegedly told Mr. Burn: "You are dreadful in the part".

Mr. Burn later commented on the incident to Christopher Matthews – and on Monday he applied for an order to be brought against Mr. Connor.

I learnt Mr. Burn was also involved in an earlier incident with the director of the production.

This happened before it opened when the actor complained that he needed more help because he found his role too difficult.

Tempers flared, but apologies were made later.

Mr. Connor refused to discuss the incident when I contacted him at his flat on Friday.

"You leave this story alone,' he said. "These sort of things are mere dust. I don`t want anything to do with this… I don`t wish to discuss it. It will affect the play badly. And it`s a good play that makes people laugh."

Mr. Pieter Toerien, producer of *My Fat Friend*, said the dispute was personal.

"I have had no report from the management of any misconduct committed by Mr. Connor on stage."

The second report is taken from an edition of the *Daily News*, which was published on Monday 23 July 1973:

ACTOR IN COMEDY IS FIRED

Jonathan Burn, the British actor who appeared in *My Fat Friend* opposite Kenneth Connor in Johannesburg, has been fired by Mr. Pieter Toerien. He will not be going to Durban for the show`s opening tomorrow night and a replacement will be found.

Mr. Toerien, the impresario who brought the Charles Laurence comedy to South Africa, said today that he had fired Burn "for causing an intolerable situation".

It was reported in a Sunday newspaper yesterday that a personal feud had developed between Kenneth Connor, one of the stars of the show, and Burn.

The newspaper said the two had been at loggerheads ever since the show opened.

Connor, who has acted in numerous *Carry On* films, is alleged to have told Burn to "shut up" during performance nine days ago.

The third report was published in an unknown newspaper on 24 July 1973:

FURORE OVER 'FAT FRIEND'

An angry Jonathan Burn flies back to London this morning to consult his agent after being fired from the cast of *My Fat Friend*, which opens in Durban tonight.

Mr. Burn was dismissed yesterday in a curt telegram from the show`s producer, Mr. Pieter Toerien, who also forbade the nude star of *Oh! Calcutta!* to enter Durban`s Alhambra Theatre.

Mr. Toerien flew to Durban last night – with Mr. Burn`s return air tickets to Britain – accompanied by another British actor called in to take over the part.

He is Mr. David Oxley, who was busy learning his lines as he flew from Johannesburg to join comedian Kenneth Connor and the other two members of the cast.

The drama behind the scenes of this successful British comedy erupted last week when Mr. Burn went to the police and asked for a Court order to be issued against Mr. Connor, star of the show.

"This sort of thing has never happened before," Mr. Toerien said in Durban last night. "It's unheard of in the acting profession. Burn created an intolerable situation. The rest of the cast can no longer work with him after he has taken this action against Kenneth Connor."

Mr. Burn, who arrived in Durban by train yesterday morning, expecting to appear in tonight's performance, was greeted by the telegram firing him when he got to his hotel.

It accused him of breach of contract and said he had been dismissed because his actions seriously jeopardised the production of *My Fat Friend.*

"I don't see how I can be in breach of contract for asking for police protection," Mr. Burn said last night. "I have talked briefly to my solicitors here, and I intend taking up the matter with my agent when I get back to London, when we'll decide what our next steps will be."

He claimed there had been a "conflict of convictions" between himself and Mr. Connor right from the opening of the play in Johannesburg.

The dispute came to a head at the end of the first week's performance – on stage, where, Mr. Burn alleges, Mr. Connor directed a personal remark at him during the course of the play.

He said: "Oh why doesn't he shut up," to another actor, Christopher Matthews, as we were on the stage. The remark was clearly referred to me and was not in the script."

Mr. Toerien yesterday denied any knowledge of the alleged remark. Mr. Burn accused the producer of not being in full possession of his facts.

"The comment was made to me. Connor childish to the extent of ad-libbing. It was a quite extraordinary bit of behaviour by an actor of his experience."

Mr. Toerien said Mr. Burn's action was "most unjustified, most unprofessional and totally uncalled for".

Meanwhile, Mr. Connor, veteran of more than twenty *Carry On* films (again, this number should be seventeen!), carried on with his assertion yesterday that the whole matter was "a storm in a tea cup".

Mr. Connor, who is known to be upset by the publicity, refused to comment further on the issue last night. "Just write R.I.P. to it – and forget it."

I wonder why my father never mentioned this whole episode. The only stories that came back to me via phone calls to Micky were that his hay fever allergies and sinus problems had caused breathing problems in the high altitude of Johannesburg. This resulted in him having to see the theatre doctor. An oxygen cylinder and mask, which was kept in the wings, was prescribed, and Kenny would suck on this prior to going on stage each time.

Kenny was also told off for working in this troubled country with its Apartheid regime. Equity even tried to black list him from going on the tour. The cast's security was tightly monitored by the South African producer, and whenever the cast decided they wanted to go out for a company dinner after the show, he provided them with a police riot wagon to take them to and from a steak house.

So trouble was all around Kenny on this tour and yet, out of all these dark happenings, the show was an enormous success and he received good critique.

Kenny rarely kept reviews of his work, but I found the following cutting amongst his belongings:

BRILLIANT TOUCHING COMEDY

By Tim Aitchinson

Having seen Kenneth Connor only in the *Carry On* films I found myself prejudging him to be a slap-sticky kind of actor, and – my, oh my – how wrong I was.

This man is a polished actor, and portrayed to the life the intelligent, basically lonely and sensitive homosexual.

Henry's ever-ready bitchiness, his intuitive understanding of what makes people tick, his readiness to make a razor-like stab at other people's weaknesses, but his essential human warmth – all these qualities were accurately and delightfully put across by Mr. Connor for whom I now feel great respect.

I am sure Kenny kept this review as it recognises him as an actor, a consummate actor – a serious actor. An actor and not only a 'slapstick' comic. These few words proving his worth.

Chapter Eight

Twice-Nightly

Despite some initial problems and misgivings by Kenny and the rest of the cast, the revue *Carry On London* was firstly staged at the Birmingham Hippodrome from 14 – 29 September 1973, before opening at the Victoria Place in London on 4 October 1973. The show was to run until March 1975.

The IRA was pretty active at the time and so many bomb warnings were sent to the theatre that the cast became quite complacent about it. One evening, when the call to evacuate came, Kenny and Bernie had just got changed for the Boy Scout sketch.

'Come on,' said Bernie. 'Let`s go across the road for a half.' Kenny didn't argue and Bernie led the way out of the stage door to the pub opposite. They strode in and straight up to the bar in full scout uniform, long socks and shorts and all.

'Can I have two halves of Guinness, please?' said Bernie.

'No, you`re under age!' the landlord replied. 'Now, get out!'

'I only asked,' replied Bernie, using his well-known catchphrase.

The landlord was defeated and it was one pint each on the house. The pub customers were in fits.

In March 1974, I was back at Pinewood to do a day's filming on *Carry On Dick*. Kenny was also in the film, of course. This meant that both he and the rest of the *Carry On* London cast were filming at Pinewood or on location in the daytime, as well as performing twice-nightly at the Victoria Palace. Talk about a punishing schedule!

We were shooting an exterior on the backlot and I had done my scene as a robber holding up a sedan chair. The pay-off being several Bow Street Runners emerge from the small sedan chair and surround me. The day was running slow as the weather was not playing ball with us. The sun was in and out between slow moving clouds and ruining light continuity. This scene involved Bernie Bresslaw and the glamorous Margaret Nolan, who had been robbed by Big Dick, and were both naked apart from carefully positioned coverings! Their dressing gowns had been on and off numerous times, as the clouds came and went, and there was still nothing in the can. They were frozen!

'Fair gap in the clouds coming', the lighting cameraman shouted helpfully.

'Set for a take!' said Gerald.

Everyone rushed around and the gowns were removed again.

'Turn over... and action!' called Gerald.

All was going well with the time until someone started to sing. 'Silence!' shouted Gerald angrily. 'We`re shooting. Cut!'

Chaos! Behind the set some of the cast were sitting on deckchairs trying to warm in the watery sun. Kenneth Williams had grown bored and bitchy mischief had manifested itself to singing.

'Kenneth, behave!' called Gerry.

'Well, I didn`t know,' moaned Kenneth. 'I was only trying to stay happy by singing to my fellow actors. I mean, really, there`s no pleasing some people. It`s a fucking insult, that`s what I think!'

And so it went on. But that was Kenneth – impulse, and perfect timing. The look on poor Bernie's face was one of resigned, smiling frustration. 'You bastard,' it said.

Back in 1973, ATV decided to broadcast a compilation of highlights from the *Carry On London* stage show on ITV. The programme – entitled *What a Carry On!* – was hosted by Shaw Taylor and included clips from a number of the *Carry On* films that had been made to date.

Maybe it was *What a Carry On!* that later persuaded Peter Rogers and Gerald Thomas to allow ATV to make *Carry On Laughing*. In total, thirteen one-off sitcoms were made under the prefix at ATV's studios in Borehamwood and originally shown in 1975. Kenny appeared in all but one of the historical romps. Each of these episodes are listed below:

The Prisoner of Spenda
The Baron Outlook
Orgy and Bess
One in the Eye for Harold
The Nine Old Cobblers
The Case of the Screaming Winkles
The Case of the Coughing Parrot
Under the Round Table
Short Knight, Long Daze
And in My Lady's Chamber
Who Needs Kitchener?
Lamp-Posts of the Empire

Both Sid James and Hattie Jacques were not to make any further *Carry On* films after *Carry On Dick*. Indeed, there were quite a few new cast members when Rogers and Thomas put *Carry On Behind* into production back in 1975. These included Ian Lavender, who Kenny had, of course, previously worked with on the radio series, *Parsley Sidings*. Ian still has mixed memories of working on *Behind*:

'For many reasons, *Carry On Behind* was not amongst the most successful of the collection. There was the almost requisite foul winter weather in the spring that we shot the film. We also lost actors on a number of occasions due to illness etc. In the scheme of a *Carry On* schedule, that meant hasty rewrites and cuts.

'I loved the series and was so glad to be working with so many people who had made me laugh so much over the years. I loved watching the contrast between Ken (as Major Leep) and Peter Butterworth in particular. Ken was precision itself and Peter had a much more improvisational approach. However, their differing approaches achieved the same result and neither of them wasted a moment of their or anyone else's time and effort.

'What we were taught in those days at drama school was that we would only learn by watching other actors at work. Getting a job on something like a *Carry On* film had about it an element of sinking or swimming. They didn't give you the job unless they thought you could hack it. And because of the hectic schedules, there usually wasn't time for lessons from the senior artistes. So you watched. But if you had people like Ken, Peter, and Joanie Sims to watch, you were already in a fortunate position.'

Sherrie Hewson, who also worked with Kenny on *Carry On Behind*, as well as an episode of *Carry On Laughing* called *And In My Lady's Chamber*, still has happy memories of working with Kenny:

'Kenneth was one of the greats, an underestimated actor who had brilliant comedy timing. He was a consummate professional in every way, and would have been acknowledged for his talent had he still been with us now. I found him a joy to work with. Each time it was like receiving a masterclass in the art of comic acting.'

England had one of the hottest summers on record in 1976, and with it came *Carry On England*. Kenny had a key role as Major S. Melly, a pompous commanding officer put in charge of an experimental mixed sex anti-aircraft battery somewhere in England. I played Gunner Hiscocks with a short cameo built into the script. All the exteriors were shot at Pinewood on a part of the backlot called The Orchard, as it had once been the country mansion's orchard. This was where the army camp set was built and we all spent a month in the sun playing Frisbee between takes.

Kenny had decided to play his character with the same slight speech impediment that the late General Montgomery had, and added to this a little moustache. His sergeant major was played by the fantastic Windsor Davies and they sparked off of each other really well. And with the introduction of Patrick Mower and Judy Geeson, together with other much-loved actors, we all thought it was going to be one of the best *Carry On* films in years – but we were wrong! The fun and the buzz we all had while making the film did not translate to the screen. What went wrong? Maybe too much fun and not looking at the bigger picture. Sadly, it received miserable reviews.

With the daily routine of shooting going to schedule, and the sun blazing down day after day, it was like being on a holiday in the countryside. At lunch break there was on-site catering in the orchard. There was always a roast of the day and dishes like grilled trout cooked on the barbecue, together with a massive buffet.

However, this excellent spread didn't impress Kenny in the slightest. He said, 'All you really need is a sandwich or you can't do the job'.

Kenny and Windsor used to wander through the gardens up to the studio bar and have rare roast beef sandwiches with raw onion and horseradish and halves of bitter. One day, I tagged along. You can have too much trout you know! Well, it was like going into Kenny and Windsor's local pub! They were welcomed by the staff like regulars, with conversations being continued from the day before. The TV series *Space 1999* was being filmed at the time, and soon the girls in the cast came in still wearing all their amazing make-up. All of them were stunning and soon the centre of attention!

A few years earlier, in the same bar, the producer Gerry Anderson had quizzed Kenny and a few others about wanting to make a new futuristic space series. This one, he said, would use real actors and not the fantastic puppets that we all love. He was worried whether it would translate. Would the public reject it? Their advice was that Gerry should do it. They argued that with his name on it, they are bound to watch. So, he obviously took their advice on board!

The next time we went to the bar at lunch break we found Patrick Mower there chatting up the *Space 1999* girls. If there's a hint of a female, Patrick doesn't like to miss out! One day, Patrick made a move on Judy Geeson. Judy had brought along a small camera to take some snaps, just like you would for holiday memories. She was sat in the sun on a blanket studying her camera, her little, fluffy white Maltese Terrier by her side. Patrick went over and lay down beside her. He leant on one elbow and started chatting. The dog started rogering his army boot, which he tried to ignore. The

121

dog persisted while Patrick crossed the troubled leg over the other, at the same time as chatting more expressively. The dog went with it. He tried stroking the dog's head with a hidden 'flick away' in between strokes. The little dog intensified its efforts and all the time Judy studied her camera, ignoring the situation. The stars viewed these goings on from their chairs while in suppressed hysterics. '

What's the camera, Judy?' Jack Douglas asked, trying to be friendly.

The nearby cast members told Jack to be quiet, as they were keen to see what would happen next. Judy turned and responded that it was her new one and she was trying to work out how to use it. Knowing a bit about cameras, Jack beckoned her over. Judy got up immediately and went over to Jack, leaving poor Patrick and the cute little doggie all alone and all loved-up together!

Jack was the last of the regulars to join the *Carry On* team. Because of this, he was treated like the new boy at school, and so the other 'pupils' did tease him from time-to-time.

The following day, after Jack had spoken in depth to Judy about her camera, he turned up with his. Well, not just the camera, but a case full of camera gear as well. Eyes were turned to heaven in a 'here we go again' sort of a way. He sat down, and placing his pipe in his mouth, he started unpacking the kit. There were clicks and turns and the removing and replacing of lens covers, as he locked on a huge telephoto lens and started aiming it around the set.

'Looks like a bloody great elephant's donger,' said Joan Sims, tears in her eyes.

Just then Jack was called to the set.

'Coming,' he said, cheerfully.

Jack crammed the camera with its long lens into the script compartment on the side of his chair. He then grabbed his script, stood up and marched off with great purpose. The weight of the camera was too much for the chair and it tipped over sideways onto the camera case spilling everything out.

'Silly prick,' said Joan, leading the laughter.

By the end of the filming, we privates were all pretty well trained as Kenny and Jack, and many of the others who had done National Service, taught us how to march and do the gun drill. Kenny loved putting us through the parade drill, shouting out his orders with vicious hatred. I think he was getting his own back for all those enforced army years. However, we loved our enforced training, marching and gourmet food, and not forgetting the *Space 1999* girls thrown in. You could say it was a film within a film!

My big moment on the film finally arrived when we were filming in the men's barrack room set one afternoon. It's fair to say I was quite nervous. Prior to this scene, Gerald was talking to Kenny and yours truly when the press publicity woman for the studio came over with a pretty girl. She told Gerald that the girl had won 'Miss TV Times' and part of the deal was to visit Pinewood Studios. The lady then asked him if he'd have any objections to the winner having some photos taken with some of the *Carry On* team. Gerald said that would be fine.

'Why not take a photo of her with Jeremy here?' he suggested. 'Two starlets in the making.'

Gerald turned and smiled at Kenny.

'That should annoy Mr. Mower, don't you think?!'

After the photos were taken, I returned to do my scene. As the youngest of the soldiers, I was not allowed to go through the tunnel to the girls' hut and I was left behind frustrated. Gerald made me react to my rebuff by doing Kenny's disappointed 'Cor!' This made him laugh like a drain. This is probably the reason why he made me do several takes, something normally unheard of on a *Carry On* film!

A few months later, Micky and I went to the press screening of *Carry On England* in Soho. I had invited a couple of agents along to try and impress them with my performance. As the film progressed I turned to Micky to remind her to look out for my award-winning scene.

'Here it comes,' I said.

But it didn't! Gerald came up afterwards and shook my hand.

'Sorry Jeremy, but we had shot so much material that lots had to be cut, and your scene was not crucial to the plot,' he confessed.

Oh, the embarrassment. Shit, the agents! Ah well, making the film had been huge fun with Kenny. It was a great summer, and to cap it off James Hunt won the British Grand Prix!

Kenny's second and final stage show with the *Carry On* gang was staged at the since-demolished Royal Opera House in Scarborough between June and September 1976. Described as 'A New Fun Packed Holiday Farce', *Carry On Laughing with 'The Slimming Factory'* saw Kenny appearing on stage with Jack Douglas, Peter Butterworth and Liz Fraser. *The Golden Shot*'s Anne Aston was also in the Sam Cree penned farce, which was directed by Jack Douglas' brother, Bill Roberton. Roberton's other directing credits included Sid James' farce, *The Mating Season*.

Jack had decided to stay in a caravan in the countryside on an estate. One Monday, he came into the theatre and told Kenny that he'd been out shooting on the Sunday and had done well.

'Tonight, I'm having Partridge casserole,' said Jack very proudly. 'I've prepared a brace of birds and they are in the slow cooker. A bottle of Claret breathing beside.'

'Lovely,' said Kenny.

The next night Kenny decided to quiz Jack about his meal.

'How did you get on?' he asked.

'I forgot to turn it on,' Jack replied. 'I got pissed on an empty stomach instead.'

Kenny did not exactly have a remarkable time when he was making *Carry On Emmannuelle* the following year. The only interesting incident he told me about took place between him and a motorbike cop while filming in Park Lane. Kenny played a chauffeur and in one scene had to drive around parts of London. A camera had been mounted on the wing of a limousine and he had to drive around Park Lane delivering his lines and reactions. In the back were a limited crew of director, cameraman and soundman, the latter two huddled on the floor, with Gerald squatting with his script. This was going well, considering how tricky a part of London it is to drive around, until a policeman pulled the limousine over and tried to book Kenny for driving a dangerous vehicle. Gerald, the director (the director is in charge at all times, the director is God, the director has no equal!) had by now thrown himself on top of the other two and they were all silent, hiding. Kenny was asked the usual questions.

'Are you in charge of this vehicle?' asked the policeman.

'Yes, but through my director,' quipped Kenny.

'Did you put that metal structure on the side of this vehicle?' he replied. It's a danger. It could kill someone.'

'Well, you avoided it,' replied my father.

With that the giggles and snorts began in the back.

'There is no need for that sort of remark,' the policeman went on. 'Who is your employer?'

'I'm self-employed and I do this for charity – at least that's what the producer says all the time!' said Kenny straight-faced.

By now there were hysterics and choking emanating from all three men in the back, as they tried to get up off the floor and look presentable.

'Ask him with the script,' said Kenny. 'I'm only the driver.'

Gerald had to come clean and talk his way out of it, promising not to do it again.

'You have put a stop to our filming,' he said. 'We will go.'

The policeman rode off knowing he had done his job of keeping the highways of London safe and Kenny drove the car away with Gerry knowing he had got the last shot in the can anyway!

To aid with the promotion of the VHS releases of the early *Carry On* films, including *Carry On* Nurse and *Carry On Cruising*, Kenny appeared on a couple of TV interviews. These appearances have found their way onto YouTube recently. You may be interested to know that it's these interviews, and the BBC Radio 2 series, *The Life of Kenneth Connor*, which Kenny made in the late Eighties, which compelled me to write this book! In the case of the TV interviews in particular, it's just not him, not the real Kenneth Connor. If you watch the interviews (with Viv Lumsden on BBC's *Garden Party*, and Vince Hill on Central TV's *Gas Street*) you can see how awkward it is to interview him. He's not forthcoming at all, and avoids answering the questions as much as possible. Then Kenny can be seen picking up a video box to plug the films when he's clearly had enough!

In 1992, Kenny was offered a part in *Carry On Columbus*, but was dismayed by the script and took it as an insult to be offered it. He wrote back saying he had moved on now and had been enjoying several years work with David Croft doing parts he loved that were funny. And that was that.

The *Carry On* team – both in-front and behind-the-camera – were quite a large family to cope with, and Kenny lived with them on set but very rarely socialised with them. Here are a few thoughts and some experiences he had with the team:

Sid James

Kenny and Sid had the same approach to the business of acting and came to the *Carry On* series via the same route. They both had a great deal of theatre experience, and also had a good track record of performing comedy and drama on the radio. Kenny and Sid always stuck to the script and would deliver the same performance during each take or show. Therefore it was easy for them to have a good working relationship. This is arguably one of the reasons why they worked together on radio, stage and film. Kenny took note that Sid was a troubled brother. He saw Sid's highs and lows in his professional and personal life. Kenny used to get a little concerned with Sid's gambling. Sid loved his betting and had a bit of a school going with some of the crew. If it wasn't horses, it was the dogs!

One night, as Sid and Kenny were being greeted by the usual reception of autograph hunters at the stage door of the Victoria Palace, a South African lad began to speak Sid. He mentioned quite politely that he was his nephew, and had flown over to visit. Sid just looked at him, took his show programme, signed it and walked on. Kenny was understandably shocked by this and spoke to the lad. It transpired that Sid's nephew had saved up to come and visit and backpack across Europe, and wanted to surprise him. He thought he would be greeted with open arms and taken home by his uncle. Being a stranger to London, he had no idea of where to find accommodation. Kenny took our new friend back to Home Oaks, and he stayed with us for several weeks until he got himself sorted. I wish I could remember his name. Maybe he will read this book and contact me! All I remember is he had tickets to see Roy Woods band Wizzard at the Hammersmith Odeon, and I accompanied him to this concert. Strangely, Kenny never did get to the bottom of the problem with Sid and his nephew.

Kenneth Williams

Kenny was always amazed by Kenneth`s vast knowledge and intelligence. He once came home from Pinewood and told us that Kenneth could speak numerous languages, and what he did not know about history was not worth knowing. And politics and art and literature, as well! Between 'messin' about' on set, they would have some quite in-depth conversations, debating all sorts. Kenny loved his bitchy wit. The Connor family, it must be said, find great humour in farting and its consequences, and with Kenneth`s scatological rants on the human body`s capabilities and design faults, Kenny was in hysterics most of the time. And boy, could Kenneth rant – no-one could get a word in! They say opposites attract and their domestic habits were just that. Kenneth`s home was spartan with surroundings of sterile cleanliness and nothing to get in the way. Whereas Kenny's house was full of eccentric clutter and warmth.

If Kenny sees Kenneth up in the clouds, he will find him giving Moses and all the prophets a tough ethical debate – and pouring disinfectant down all the heavenly toilets. He was often heard to say, concerning toilets, 'I put the Harpic down, and run!'

Hattie Jacques

Kenny loved Hattie, but then everyone did. In the *Carry On* family she was the aunt you could talk to. The listening post for all problems. Kenny had always had a problem with dancing, and Hattie tried to help him out. Hattie was, of course, a large lady, but she moved so delicately on her agile ballerina dainty feet. She was amazing to watch, but it did not further Kenny's abilities in the dancing world. 'Keep practising, Kenny,' she used to say, smiling and raising her eyes to heaven.

Even I thought of her as an aunt. Whenever I visited Pinewood, Thames or ATV, she would always have time for me. 'Hello Jeremy, come and tell me what you've been up to,' she used to say.

Kenny just loved working with her. 'She is an angel,' he would recall. I bet she's up there in heaven still desperately trying to teach Kenny to dance!

Bernard Bresslaw

Apart from an advert for Murray Mints, Kenny did not work with Bernie until *Carry On Up the Jungle*. When they appeared in *Stop it Nurse* together, Kenny told me at the time that he did not like Bernie's timing. 'He

129

jumps in on a line too early and kills the gag,' he said. To be fair, I think everyone wanted to belt through that lame show, but by the end of the season Kenny had nothing but good to say about his acting skills.

Bernie and Kenny worked together quite a lot in theatre, and one thing Kenny came to know is that you'd rarely see Bernie around during the day when on tour. If you wanted to get hold of him, you just went to the nearest library. Bernie was an avid bookworm and when he had a book in his hand he was totally absorbed, the manuscript just three inches from his face. His eyesight was worse than Kenny's and they both found their way about the set by sixth sense!

I acted in Sheridan's *The Rivals* with Bernie and he would talk about touring with Kenny:

> 'We called that last tour the "Gourmet Tour". We would meet up each lunch time and go to a different eatery. We took it in turns to find a restaurant and surprise each other. It was great fun touring around England like two old thespians indulging.'

Peter Butterworth

Peter and Kenny got on famously. They were like-minded and enjoyed each other's company. They worked together on film and in theatre, but again only socialised when at work. They both had war time experiences and were great family men. It is amazing they were not best mates considering.

Chapter Nine

Pantomania

In 1982, Kenny joined Ian Lavender in a new touring production of Shaw's *Getting Married*. The cast included Barbara Leigh Hunt, Frank Middlemass and Andrew Cruickshank. Ian can still vividly remember the three months he spent with Kenny during the tour:

'We opened at The Malvern Festival Theatre and sat in the garden through those balmy spring days, played the show at night and then watched Alex Higgins win the world snooker championship late at night.

'I spent a lot of my time with Ken on that tour, travelling together and often staying in the same digs/pubs/flats and an occasional hotel. My memories seem to be of what we did before and after performances. For example, we sat in little restaurants overlooking The Mumbles and the Malvern Hills, just talking, talking and talking. I have to suppose, therefore, that there were an awful lot of stories exchanged in those evenings and an awful lot of laughter. Jeremy joined us for some of those weeks and I hope that he recollects similarly. It still remains one of the happiest jobs in my life.

'We both were married to ladies known as Micky, and he always referred to his as "My Micky". But although he talked of her freely, you all knew that home was home and private.

'*Getting Married* is not the easiest of pieces, but Ken gave one of the most sensitive and understated performances you could ever wish to see or be a part of. It made me, and a lot of other people beside, wish we had seen more of this side of Kenneth Connor, the stage actor.'

Kenny's panto days started early. His first appearances in the genre were on TV. In 1957, he appeared in the BBC pantomime, *Pantomania: Babes in the Wood*. The amazing cast included Eamonn Andrews, Sam Costa, Charlie Drake, Tony Hancock, Benny Hill, Sid James, Bill Maynard, Sylvia Peters and Ted Ray. Imagine assembling a cast like that now for TV – let alone the stage!

In 1965, he played one of the Robbers with Sid James in *Babes in the Wood* at the London Palladium. Singer Frank Ifield topped the bill as Robin Hood, while he was ably supported by Arthur Askey, as 'Big Hearted Martha', and Roy Kinnear, as Nicholas the Sherriff's page. The Aida Foster Children featured a young Elaine Paige and Sharon Arden, now better known as Sharon Osborne. The book was by David Croft, who would go on to co-write episodes of *'Allo 'Allo!* and *Hi-de-Hi!* that Kenneth would appear in.

Kenny then returned to the London Palladium in 1969 to appear in *Dick Whittington*. This time singer Tommy Steele topped the bill. Support also came from Mary Hopkin and Billy Dainty. Research shows that a young David Essex was also in this cast and understudied Tommy Steele. Essex was given the opportunity to perform the role at certain performances.

Kenny also appeared in Aladdin at the New Victoria Theatre. David Hamilton, Adrienne Posta (who played opposite Kenny in *Carry On Behind*), Sally James and Christopher Beeny all starred.

In Christmas 1978, Kenny appeared in the panto *Jack and the Beanstalk* at the Watersmeet Theatre, Rickmansworth. Peter Byrne, who appeared briefly in

Carry On Cabby, joined Kenny in the cast alongside Jess Conrad, Arnold Ridley and Cardew Robinson, who is best remembered now for playing the Fakir in *Carry On Up the Khyber*.

Back in the Eighties, BBC radio used to produce a panto, and Kenny took part in Aladdin in 1980 and Sleeping Beauty in 1983.

But there are two pantomimes that I particularly want to recall. Firstly, a production of Cinderella at Bristol in 1983. It was an exciting re-entry into theatre. After seven years I was going to be back on stage again. We rehearsed in a Greek Orthodox Church in Ladbroke Grove, and took our lunch break at the nearest pub, which was yet another dive. They allowed drugs to be sold in the tiled corridor that ran between the two bars and the toilets. There was even a set of gram scales to measure out the dope. Fair trading really. Gave it an air of legality.

Lionel Blair was contacted to play Buttons, as well as to direct the production. Kenny and Victor Spinetti were set to play the Ugly Sisters, while the role of Prince Charming had been given to the sultry siren of soap TV, Kate O'Mara. Playing opposite, Dandini (Charming's side kick) would be Paula Wilcox of *Man About the House* fame. As for me? Well, I was due to be an ASM and a Villager etc.!

Rehearsals were going well with lots of energy and fun – that was until day four when Kate O'Mara was admitted to hospital with a migraine! When this was announced in the rehearsal room, there were various exchanged glances and not much else but silence. Lionel, at the director's desk, looked shocked and angry at the same time.

'Right,' said Lionel, with purpose. 'I'm going to ring my sister.'

With that, Lionel stormed off in search of a phone. Kenny, sizing up the situation, grabbed hold of Victor.

'Let's rehearse the bedroom routine,' he suggested. The choreographer rounded up the dancers and they started working out at the far end of the hall.

Lionel was back in twenty minutes and made the announcement that his sister Joyce had just got home from shopping in Brent Cross and would join rehearsals after lunch. Rehearsals were brought to a halt and we retired to the drug pub for sandwiches and pints of Guinness.

'I knew she wouldn't last,' said Kenny, sipping his Guinness. 'She was scared stiff looking at this bunch of variety turns'.

'What's Joyce going to be like though?' I asked.

'You'll see,' Kenny laughed loudly. 'Now, another half?'

Joyce bustled into the rehearsal room with a large handbag on her shoulder and still clutching her Fenwick's shopping bags. She was a whirlwind. The whole room came alive, like summer had blown into this dank winter rehearsal hall. How could I have thought that the silent, pensive O'Mara was the way to go!

'Fuck me. That was a bit sudden,' said Joyce, throwing her bags down by Lionel's desk.

There was laughter and kisses all round. Now this is what pantomime is all about, I thought, looking at Kenny who had a knowing smile on his face!

From then on it was like being at home with the Blairs. The rest of the rehearsals went well, with Paula's performance really lifting now that she had an amazing fun-loving Prince Charming. We all said our goodbyes at the church hall, and looked forward to reconvening at the Bristol Hippodrome.

When going on tour, you spend the rehearsals attempting to suss out who you think would be suitable to share digs with. Working and living together with some neurotic alcoholic actor ruins a happy tour! Did I hear a cynical laugh? Kenny had made various phone calls to find accommodation and we had both warmed to the other ASM, Henry Tomlinson, who's the son of actor, David Tomlinson (*Mary Poppins*, *Bedknobs and Broomsticks*). He was every bit like his father; very, very English and public school. If he tried a cockney accent it was as bad as Dick Van Dyke's chimney sweep! He was a great laugh, though, very tall and drove an old Jag XJ6 and wore brown brogues, which he kept in shoe trees overnight.

The fourth member of our digs was the sound engineer, Alan Sharma. He turned out to be a good contact if you needed batteries or condoms! Alan had to have a huge supply of condoms to cover the battery packs of the personal microphones. This stopped body sweat from damaging the equipment. He used to cause all sorts of embarrassment and blushes to chemist assistants when placing his large orders. Especially when he would say, 'Hurry up, please. I`ve got a busy night!'

The digs that Kenny found were two floors of a regency school house belonging to a housemaster of Clifton College. It was up high, just outside central Bristol in the village of Clifton, a sort of suburb. We all had our own rooms, three in the basement which had a communal kitchen, dinner lounge, bathroom and bedrooms off. Kenny had a first floor room. It was a large detached stone building, with a massive black front door and bay windows either side. A grand residence for pantomime performers. He was looking forward to this venture. It was like going back to his roots for him and a reminder of his Bristol Old Vic days.

We checked in at the house on a Sunday evening, prior to rehearsals on stage the following morning. We threw everything into our rooms and put a previously prepared chilli, made by Micky, in the fridge.

'Dad, let's go and take a look at the theatre,' I suggested.

Henry joined us and we all jumped in his Jag and drove the short distance to the Hippodrome. It was the first time I'd been backstage for many a year and it felt like going home after imprisonment. The stage was bustling with the crew moving in the scenery and flying the cloths. I saw this tall, red-haired woman wearing a head scarf and white lace fingerless mittens walking a sixteen foot flat on to the stage.

'Bloody Hell – she's strong,' I said.

'That's Simon, mid-sex change,' said a passing crew member. 'He's a bit sensitive at the moment and prefers to be called Simone.'

He made a nod with a protective concerned look and carried on across the stage.

The crew were taking a break and we were cordially invited to join them for a drink in the pub opposite stage door. We entered The Grapes of Wrath and Kenny offered a round, which was declined. They already had a fresh round in. I had a pint of lager and Kenny a Guinness – ebony and ivory. We sat with the crew. Simon (Simone) was at the table, her laced hand clasping a pint, her hand dwarfed the pint glass as she brought it up to her lips. I gazed at her, the orange red curly fly away hair and big jaw, and then saw the beard stubble piercing through the white pan make-up. She gave up theatre after the final op. and took up a new job as a secretary. I hope she is settled now. She was also the lighting desk operator – no mean task – but her insular attitude was, well, unnerving!

'Stand by LX cue 7,' I said. 'Hello Simon? Are you there?'

'Yes I am,' she said. 'And of course I'm standing by. Oh, and the name is Simone.'

'Whoops!' I replied, somewhat embarrassed. 'LX cue 7 – Go.'

No *Cinderella* production can be without the Broker's Men. They were in the play to extract debts from Baron Hardup, the father of Cinderella, and his step daughters. In this case, Lionel had cast a double act from Southport, near Liverpool – The Jolly Brothers. They were so stunned to be working with all the stars, that their naivety brought so much colour to the production. One day we had a weird conversation.

'Fuckin' hell, Jeremy, how do you live with your dad?' he asked 'It must be weird.'

'He's my dad. I don't understand the question.'

'Wow! Fuckin' amazing!'

These guys were very, very funny and in a way stole the show. Lots of the cast used to stand in the wings watching their routines. The panto script was predictable, of course, but they put their mark on it.

The panto was a huge success and a lavish production. It had amazing sets and lighting. The costumes were by David and Elizabeth Emmanuel, and featured lots of gorgeous satin and embroidery. I'm sure Princess Diana would rather have worn this stuff for her wedding!

During the final rehearsals it was decided by Lionel that dear Henry was not good enough to play the part of Major Domo. The Major Domo is a sort of MC in *Cinderella*, who announces the guests to the ball. He could not bang the staff on the floor and then speak the lines, but could only do it simultaneously so could not be heard. He was demoted to playing Darth Vader in the Ugly Sisters' bedroom scene, as the poor so and so couldn't seem to co-ordinate the swinging of the light saber. This used to annoy Lionel no end, so I inherited the Major Domo part and spoke my first words on stage for a long time.

Once the show was under way, it was like a factory process. It was twelve shows a week, and the cast and crew were occupied from about one o'clock in the afternoon until eleven o'clock at night. Normal activities held outside these hours consisted of eating, sleeping and looking for the next job!

Kenny became quite fatigued after the first few weeks. He didn't want to do panto really. He was just paying the bills. After the twelfth show on Saturday night, we would drive back to our respective homes together, and then off again to Bristol on Monday morning.

Kenny contacted his younger brother, Ron, who lived in Dorset, invited him over to Bristol for a reunion and to meet his nephew, whom he had not seen for at least twenty years. Ron had been a respected GP in Liphook, Hants., but for health reasons was now retired and occupied himself with writing poetry and drinking Holsten Pils! We met at the stage door between shows and went to the pub. God he sounded like Kenny, but he had a superior air about him – which I'm sure was there to prove his worth over a famous brother!

My uncle saw the second show and, after a drink, we went back to the digs, where I prepared a midnight feast. This is part of the theatre routine. You finish your day's work and go and eat your evening meal. It's just about six hours out of kilter from the normal working day as any shift worker will tell you. Boiled potatoes,

Surprise peas and lamb chops, the rind pasted with Dijon mustard. A jus of red wine reduction and sour cream, and several glasses of the same red wine. I think the feast finished at four in the morning! I sat and listened to them exchanging their boyhood stories about Ron's time in the navy and Kenny's in the army. It was brilliant and quite moving.

Next day my uncle, Kenny and I went for a noon pub lunch in Clifton and I soon realised that after the first half of Guinness, Kenny was pissed! Ron was consummate in his behaviour and chatted with humour through lunch.

We arrived at the theatre shortly after the half hour call, which had the company manager a little worried, as we were never late. Upon seeing Kenny, he immediately brought a nice strong cup of coffee to his dressing room. The matinee performance was of great amusement to the cast, and they wondered if he was 'pissed'! He got through the show – I don't think the audience noticed – and slept in his dressing room between shows.

Ron and I went for a drink in a sort of disco/wine bar that the female dancers used to frequent. It was a safe place for girls to go to, because it doubled as a sort of a gay bar.

'Why is your father always so emotional?' asked Ron. 'He always overdoes things. Life is life, Jeremy. You have to make a meal out of it.'

'Mmm, I guess he is overwhelmed by this meeting up,' I said. 'I haven't seen him like this for ages. Anyway, good to meet you again!'

We clinked glasses, and my uncle drained his glass dry.

'Why do you two drink large ports between shows?' he asked.

'It's become a Connor tradition,' I replied.

'Two more Southamptons please,' Ron proclaimed.

My uncle left the next day after hugging his brother. Kenny used to meet up with him in their home town of Portsmouth now and again. He died in a hotel room in New York, quite alone, I believe.

Kenny rallied around after a few days and we started living in each other's pockets again, but everyone was beginning to tire. Everyone was getting flat. Enter the Jolly Brothers, who exclaimed, 'We're going to have a party after the show'.

They had hired an apartment in a Regency Terrace, the typical, beautiful white crescent block with black railings. The musical director had rented accommodation above them, ensuring there was a piano to go with it. Alan Bence was a live wire musician, built like a whippet, with sandy coloured hair, a cockney accent and a stammer that he put to very good use.

'W-W-When you 'avin the party then?' Alan asked.

'Oh, Saturday night of course,' said a Jolly.

'You can't f-f-fucking do that you t-t-twats,' replied Alan. 'Everyone goes back to the smoke on a Saturday night.'

One Sunday we didn't go home. Instead, Kenny, Alan and I ended up in a famous old cider house, The Celebration Tap, up near Clifton Suspension Bridge. We had been on a long walk and didn't get into the pub until about one thirty pm. Enjoying some fast pints and chatting away, we heard last orders being called out. Shit, two o'clock closing! We quickly got some rounds in. When it got to about half-past-two we realised that the pub was slowly starting to empty.

'Right, that's your lot,' shouted the landlord. 'Haven't you got homes to go to?'

The landlord came over to our table while Alan was in the middle of a yarn. The publican looked straight at him and rudely told him off for ignoring his orders to drink up. Worse still, he did this while wagging his finger at him. Alan just looked at him with a straight face.

'D-d-don't you p-p-point that thing at me,' he told him. 'It might go off!!'

We burst out laughing in uncontrollable hysterics. The landlord turned on his heel and disappeared out the back of the bar. He never came back. Alan finished his tale and we finished our drinks at leisure. We put our glasses on the counter and, after upending our chairs onto our table, we quietly left. Kenny knocked off the snicket on the door latch and pulled the door firmly shut, hearing it lock.

So, the Jolly Brothers' party had to be organised. Kenny, Alan and I went to their dressing room for a meeting. It was decided that a Thursday night was best as it was mid-week, and it was hoped that would revive a flagging cast.

'We've got to make it simple,' said Kenny. 'How's about steaks, jacket potatoes and salads? Jeremy's a good cook, he can do it!'

'Sounds great,' said the Jolly Brothers. 'Are you sure that's okay, Jeremy?'

Kenny volunteered me because I'd spent the last four years of my life in catering, but hardly as a chef though! Twenty odd steaks, all 'cook to order', was a bit daunting. We gave out our invitations, stating the half past eleven starting time, and attached a steak order list; rare, medium rare, etc. On the day, all salads were prepared up front, spuds scrubbed and ready for the oven. Kenny went to the butcher in Clifton and bought the steaks.

After curtain down, Henry whizzed me round to the Jolly Brothers to get the cooking started, while he belted back to do the after show clear up. I forgot about the timing of the spuds! Stupid! It was twelve-thirty already, but everyone told tales to the party, while I cooked the steaks to order. The feast happened and was a success. Everyone replete, a spontaneous sing-song happened. Beautiful voices singing Christmas songs.

'We need the piano,' enthused Alan.

The upright piano was then moved down one floor from his pad, with great caution, and we found him a chair. And off we went, rocking it. At two o'clock we got a knock on the door from an annoyed neighbour. Apologies were made.

'Wanker,' said Alan.

The company then gathered around the piano at Alan's request. He pressed one note and all knew what to sing – 'Silent Night'. Despite our singing, Alan received an apology from the disgruntled neighbours the following morning!

Shortly after 'Silent Night', one of the cast came up to me looking concerned.

'Your dad has left,' said the actor. 'He told me he had to go home, and was a bit weird'.

Well, we were all a bit weird. It turned out that someone had spiked the steaks with dope while I was pulling the spuds out of the oven. I was enjoying myself hugging the girls, but I had to make sure Kenny was okay. I left and headed back to the digs. He was not there. Shit! He's got lost, I thought. I left the house and wandered around looking for him. Bearing in mind I was not in a good state either, it was a marvel I found him. He was standing on one of the stanchions of the Clifton Suspension Bridge, ready to fly. I talked him down.

'I don't know what I'm doing here,' he said.

There was more to that than just being on the bridge. I walked him home and put him to bed and crashed out myself. I took him a cup of tea in the morning.

'Here you are, hot cuppa. You okay?' I asked.

'Yeah, yeah,' he assured me. 'Can you hear lions?'

Bloody hell, one hit of dope and it's scuppered him, I thought.

'What do you mean – lions?' I replied. 'Do you want some water, let's go for a walk.'

Then I heard the lion. Our digs were right by Bristol Zoo.

We only had a couple of weeks to go now. The following Saturday we decided to go home to London, taking most of our possessions with us. It's amazing what you amass on a long season away, what with visits to antique shops and book shops. Basically, it was impulse buying before going in to do the shows. I drove, as Kenny was so tired.

On the way up the M4, we spotted Lionel ahead in his Mitsubishi Colt. Suddenly, his reverse lights went on and the car swerved violently. The reverse lights went out and the car levelled up again. Fatigue. We used to wind the windows down and get a blast of cold air. Play music loud and sing along.

As often happens at the end of a tiring run, pranks started to happen, as did mistakes! We had some white Shetland ponies that towed Cinderella's coach for the spectacular ending to Act One. Joyce used to take off her princely hat, with its plume of long feathers, and tickle the ponies' willies with it. Often the ponies would go on stage with raging hard-ons!

One show, when I was standing in the wings waiting for my cue to hand Dandini (Paula Wilcox) her sword, I just stood there watching her and didn't do a damned thing! She marched off stage and ripped the sword out of my hands. When she had finished the sword routine with Joyce, she threw it off stage, right at me. I felt so bad. Concentration totally gone. Kenny never made a cock-up. Actually, he had a tough time of it. Victor Spinetti had become ill shortly into the run and had worked the rest of the season with the understudy. This meant that a lot of weight was on his shoulders.

The stage crew performed an 'Alternative Panto' one night after the audience had all gone home. The cast hurriedly changed and brought drinks down into the auditorium, the crew re-set the stage and got into costume. We roared with laughter at their production, full of parody, impersonations and in-jokes.

On the penultimate Saturday night, we were invited to an end of run party by the Bristol Old Vic Company, as it coincided with their end of production too. It was held in their scenery dock. A massive area with half-finished backcloths hanging there, like huge oil paintings. Fabulous art. It was a ticket entry affair, which paid for the food and drink. Kenny loved it and chatted about his days at the Vic.

A mate of mine had come to see the show that night. He was the son of Ken's neighbour in Harrow, and had come with a rugby team friend of his. They had made a full day of it, ending up with seeing the evening show. I had bought them tickets for the party, and by the time they got there, they were in a very festive mood. They were chatting up the girls, when they suddenly spotted a large wicker basket piled high with Satsuma oranges. Soon a massive orange fight was underway, but fortunately there was no lasting damage to the artwork.

Last night parties are always emotive events. Confessions are made, tears flow and love is professed.

'I never did like him, I'm glad it's over.'

'I love you, you know.'

'Why didn't you say that at the start of the run?'

'Here's my number, ring me!'

'Where do you live?'

'Bolton.'

'Ah well!'

Everyone was asking each other what they were doing next. The results were very diverse and random. Cruise ship shows, West End musicals, pole dancing in Tangiers, modelling, going to look after my mum, signing on and decorating the flat, but mostly, uncertainty.

Kenny, like many actors, never said goodbye. He used to tell me, 'You just don't say that. Always say "See you next time" or "See you at the Exchange," meaning the Labour Exchange.'

Anyway, after the final show, everyone was rushing for trains or lifts, and the crew were busy 'striking' the set. Kenny had this ritual for a last night, which I used to follow. After putting on his make-up, he packed it all away with the make-up towels. Toiletries from the sink were packed in and the many good luck cards removed from around his mirror. The room started to look as barren as the day we arrived. Kenny always asked for each costume to be taken away after it had been finished with. The last thing to be packed was the tea mug, so by the time you came back from curtain call all you had to do was change into civvies, grab your bag and go! He never bothered washing the make-up off. Besides, by that point it had faded due to him sweating and not touching it up during the show. Kenny also held the record for being first out of the stage door, fading into the night. It was time to go home, back to normality for a while, until the next venture! The next mission!

After the 1983 panto in Bristol, Kenny was hoping to slow up a bit at the age of 64. However, the same production company offered him *Jack and the Beanstalk* at the Richmond Theatre, in west London. The real selling point was that it was only a twenty minute drive from home. I tagged onto this production, as I'd worked for Triumph Productions quite a bit in the past. This was due to Kenny's excellent negotiating skills!

Rehearsals took place in a Territorial Army base in Wandsworth, which was within sniffing distance of Young's Brewery. From day one, it was obvious that this was going to be a far less superior production than the Lionel Blair panto of the previous year. The cast stacked up though. Suzanne Danielle (who played opposite Kenneth in *Carry On Emmannuelle*) had been cast as Jack, and Kenny as Dame. There was set to be strong support from Joan Sims as Fairy Sweetcorn, and Keith Barron as a baddy. Comedian Peter Goodwright had been brought in to play Simple Simon, and the great Jimmy Edwards had been handed the role of King. It all bode well.

We all hung around the rehearsal hall on day one chatting and catching up. The director was, well, not the best and actually had no direction. We waited and waited and nothing positive came from this director. He sauntered around in an off-white suit with a red carnation (like the war correspondent John Simpson on a day out!) speaking privately to all the stars.

'What routines do you know?' he asked. 'What song would you like to sing?'

There was no construction in place and he'd obviously not planned a bloody thing! Kenny was very quiet that day and did not seem bothered. The hall was attached to a bar, and he retired to it.

'I'll be in here if you want me,' he said casually.

It was not like Kenny at all.

Keith Barron came up to greet me.

'Hello love, what the fuck's going on?' he asked.

'I'm so glad to be working with your dad, it's great.'

Keith puffed on his Silk Cut reflectively before speaking again.

'So, Jeremy, who's playing the other half of the cow?'

Other half of the cow?! What's he on about? I was confused and then the word 'negotiation' hit me in the forehead. Keith could see I was shocked!

'Keith, would you like to come and have a drink with me and dad and find out what's going on?' I asked.

'Well, okay duck, hope I haven't upset the applecart.'

Keith, by the way, can get away with murder by using his gentle soft northern accent. But he's also a hard man when it comes to professionalism, just like Kenny was.

'What's this about a cow, dad?,' I asked. 'I thought I was going to be comic relief?'

'Ah well,' said Kenny, realising he had to come clean. 'I was going to tell you about that. Drinks?'

We talked and soon realised we were on our own. No director. Nothing but a weak script, which made poor Joanie Sims decidedly nervous. She was scared about doing live shows again after so much film and TV work. Jimmy Edwards was not there.

'I'll come when I bloody well want to,' was the message we received from the entertainer.

We were joined in the bar by the company manager, Tony Cundell. Tony was 'Mr. Touring Theatre'. He was a walking history of music hall and variety.

'Look, we need to get some front cloth routines into play,' he said with great authority. 'I've got heaps in store.'

We all cheered up and started to work on the routines. They were old, but they worked. After a week of rehearsals, we were quite polished. Still, the director had done nothing about the cow. Keith Barron was getting angry about this.

'Jeremy, go and ask him about the cow,' he pleaded. 'I don't understand why he's not doing anything about it. After all, the cow is the most important part of the panto!!'

I asked and was told that we were not ready for that yet. Kenny overheard this remark and said that at least we should select the other half of the cow. He strolled over to the dancers with purpose.

'Right, who wants to be part of Daisy?' he asked. 'You get to be in some of the routines, too'.

Quick as a flash a slim, fit Scouser stepped forward and spoke up.

'Great, I've been waiting for a break!' he said.

This was Jonathan (Jonny) Cross, a Young Generation dancer, who really wanted to do comedy. So the cow was formed. Because I had inherited two left feet from Kenny, I became the front end of the cow, so that Jono could follow my so-called dance moves if I cocked up! That way it would still manage to look wonderful.

Here's how Jono remembers his time in the panto:

'After a few years of dancing and singing in shows, I got my first acting job. Okay, it was being a cow in pantomime, but I was at least offered this chance 'to act' in Jack and the Beanstalk at the Richmond Theatre. Joining me in the skin was Jeremy. I was nervous when I first met him, as his dad was a legend in my eyes!

'When the first days of rehearsals started, we had a script-reading round a large table. Joan Sims, Susan Danielle, Susan Maughan, Keith Barron, Peter Goodwright, Jimmy Edwards, Jeremy and, of course, the great man himself, Kenneth Connor. I felt like a real actor! Yes, I know I was only a cow, and the back-end at that! But Ken didn't think that, he was supportive to our vision of 'cow acting' and encouraged us with our ideas on how to bring Daisy to life, usually over a large glass of red wine or occassionally a mug of tea!

'After a few days of rehearsals, the director would go through the various scenes but, to the cow's disappointment, every time Daisy made an entrance, the director would offer no encouragement.

"Cow on, bit of business, cow off," was all he said.

'After a few more days of this, Ken stopped the man in his tracks.

"Dicky, don't you think it's about time the boys went through the scenes with the rest of us? They are actors as well, and let's face it, Daisy is the bloody important one in this show. Jack sells the sodding cow and the kids are going to have an emotional ride watching this cow act, if you give the boys a bloody chance!"

'From that moment on, with Ken's belief and confidence in us, and sharing his knowledge and wisdom, Jez and Jono became the 'best pantomine cow in the business'.

'Kenneth Connor: a top man and a top actor, who became a friend. Jeremy and I have remained close friends ever since.'

Another actor to join in the routines was Graham Cole, who is best-known in the UK for having appeared in *The Bill* as PC Tony Stamp. So, the show slowly started to come together, but the process was far from easy.

One night the phone rang at Home Oaks and Kenny got up to answer it. Joanie Sims was on the line. She`d had a panic attack about the prospect of doing live performances again. Kenny soothed her nerves and she turned up at rehearsals the next morning as normal. When she spotted Kenny, she went over to him and gave him a big hug.

Jack and the Beanstalk opened on Friday 14 December 1984 and it was well received. We all relaxed and settled into the run. Kenny and I took turns to drive. I was living a couple of miles away in Wealdstone and we did the car share week on, week off. We`d get to Richmond for one pm, park up and go straight to a pub for sandwiches and a pint before doing the two thirty pm show.

Not long into the run, Kenny kept telling me he was getting more and more tired. He took to sleeping in his dressing room between shows instead of going out to eat. Kenny told me this was going to be his last pantomime. He had done so much panto and this was one too many. The truth is, he didn't really feel part of it.

It wasn't long before Jimmy Edwards left due to illness. Worse still, Suzanne Danielle`s lack of professionalism bugged Kenny. She often wouldn`t arrive at the theatre until the five minute call, as she had been clubbing until the early hours in the West End. You had to be in the theatre before the half hour call. That was the rule of theatre. In the old days, the company manager would dock your wages if the rule was broken. So Kenny's training bucked at this lack of respect. Suzanne was good, though, and enjoyed herself to the max both on and off the stage. Both Daisy and Jack worked well together and I'm pleased to say the kids loved us!

Jack and the Beanstalk ended on the first Saturday of February, and there was a great buzz backstage. Keith Barron had bought a bottle of champagne for each dressing room and Kenny was prancing around and making a nuisance of himself in the dressing rooms. He was so happy it was finally coming to an end.

We went to the Cobwebs Pub in between shows and, while there. we noticed Jimmy Edwards' dresser come in and take a prearranged bucket of ice away with him. What's going on? There's no Jim! Or is there?! We finished our drinks and headed back to the theatre to find that Jim had decided to come and do the last night. Tony Cundell had known about this for some time. He told Kenny that Jim was going to do some of his old routine and not stick to the script. Nothing new there then! We all prepared for the show to give it our all for the very last time. It was a full house and the Triumph Productions bosses were all going to be out front.

When it got to Jimmy's spot the entire cast were crammed into the wings to watch. He started with his penny whistle.

'I will now show you the three ways to play the penny whistle,' he said.

First, Jimmy played it the conventional way and then he stuck it up one nostril and closed the other nostril with his free finger. He then played the song again. The adults roared and the kids squealed.

'Now, the third way!' he told the intrigued last night crowd.

Jimmy turned his back to the audience and offered up the whistle to his backside. He held it there for a moment, grinning at the audience.

'Better not try that,' he laughed. 'I've just eaten.'

Then Jimmy tucked the whistle into his robes and reached for his trombone and belted out the 'Flight Of The Bumblebee'. It was brilliant. There then followed a lecture on the history of the trombone in true *Wacko!* form, before he demonstrated the range of the instrument from the very deep reverberating lows, right up to the very top. When he reached the top note, he held it for what seemed like an age and then stopped and bowed. Huge round of applause!

'Ladies and gentlemen, boys and girls,' he continued. 'When I played that top note, you couldn't fit a tram ticket between the cheeks of my arse!'

The theatre went ballistic!

'Ah well,' he said, as he looked up to the producers' box. 'I didn't want to work for Triumph Productions again anyway'.

With that, Jimmy marched off the stage to his dressing room, got changed and was driven home. He didn't even do the curtain call. Kenny was in two minds about this whole episode, but the look in his eyes said that he wish he'd thought of that!

And that was that. It was all over and time to go home. There is something of an imbalance in doing panto when you are home-based. You do the shows and go home to your private world. When you're away and co-habiting in digs in a strange town, a camaraderie usually occurs. And that makes the panto world feel like a far better place.

Chapter Ten

The Sitcom Years

As I'm sure you know, Kenny was no stranger to making appearances on TV in comedy programmes. His early sketch show, and sketch appearances, over the years included playing various roles in the 1956 series, *A Show Called Fred*, which included Peter Sellers and Graham Stark in the cast, and *The Idiot Weekly. Price 2d*. He also joined his former *Carry On Sergeant* love interest, Dora Bryan, in the BBC series, *According to Dora*, in 1968 and 1969.

In the latter years, Kenny appeared in Ted Rogers' Yorkshire TV special, *Ted On the Spot*. This was first shown on the ITV network in April 1979. He supported Ted alongside Benny Hill sidekick, Henry McGee, Peter Butterworth's wife, Janet Brown, and erstwhile *Carry On England* colleague, Diane Langton.

Kenny also made appearances in sketches featured on certain editions of Ted's long-running game show, *3-2-1!* And strangely, given their history, Kenny appeared on Frankie Howerd's 1980 Yorkshire TV special, *Frankie Howerd Reveals All*.

Kenny was also no stranger to the world of sitcom. He joined Bob Monkhouse in series two of *My Pal Bob*, in the Sixties, and played Gussie Sissons in twelve episodes of *On the House* between 1970 and 1971. The latter starred John Junkin, Derek Griffiths, Robin Askwith and Patrick Troughton. Then, of course, he appeared in the 1971 one-off festive sitcom called *All This and Christmas Too*. Written by Sam Cree, who also wrote the farce, *Stop it Nurse*, the special saw my Kenny playing opposite Sid James, Beryl Mason, Joe Gladwin and Janet Webb. He later popped up in an episode of Mollie Sugden's popular Yorkshire TV sitcom, *That's My Boy!*, in 1986.

Someone must have been listening to Kenny's vocalised wish to do more TV again, because at the same time he was approached by the BBC to join the sitcom *'Allo, Allo!'* He was surprised, as he had not done any work for BBC Light Entertainment TV since the sitcom *Room At the Bottom* in 1967. Kenny had been asked to do a second series, but had turned it down and the doors of BBC TV remained shut until David Croft asked him to be the funeral director for Rene's funeral. He took it, and so started his journey with The Croft Empire. He was soon part of the family and very much at home. The BBC rehearsal rooms were a twenty-minute drive away in North Acton, with the weekly recording at BBC Television Centre. Kenny had totally fallen on his feet again, and his wishes had come true.

Kenny had a lot of fun making *'Allo Allo'*, even during the twenty-six episode run (usually a series consisted of between six and ten episodes) when a permanent set had to be built at BBC Elstree. The only part he did not approve of was the hierarchy that developed in the rehearsal rooms. The read-through of each episode happened on a Monday morning and a long line of tables were set up with a 'T' at the top. The 'T' was for the producer, director and writers and the cast sat down the line. Gordon Kaye and Carmen Silvera made a point of sitting opposite each other nearest to the top of the 'T'. The stars nearest the producer, you see!

'What a load of shit,' Kenny complained to me. 'Who do they think they are?! We're all equal in this. We are part of one of David's repertory companies.'

'Where do you sit?' I asked.

'Right down the end,' he told me. 'I just tell them I want to smoke.'

David Croft's favoured place for all location filming was Norfolk. *Dads Army* and *You Rang, M`Lord?* were both shot there. In *'Allo, 'Allo!*, the village square of Nouvion was filmed in the courtyard of a hall near to Thetford. When a funeral barge was needed for Monsieur Alfonse, the Norfolk Broads were used. The episode was called 'The Nouvion Oars' and Alfonse's barge was needed as part of a plan to help the British airmen escape. Plans had been made to have someone steer the boat out of vision, with Kenny pretending to drive. But, of course, Kenny could handle a motor boat and he did the scene unaided. During rehearsals, an argument started on how to 'shoot' the scene. Kenny was told over his on-board radio transmitter to stay out on the water while the problem was sorted. The argument went on and on and he got bored. So he turned off the communications device and headed off downstream for a cruise, quite contented. Problem solved in the production department, they all looked out on to the broad to see an empty water! Panic set in until he returned, asking if they were ready.

One of the pleasing aspects of writing this book has been the willingness of a number of Kenny's former colleagues on *'Allo 'Allo!* to share their memories of Kenny. So here they are. I hope they go to show just how much Kenny was respected by his colleagues:

<u>Vicki Michelle (Yvette Carte-Blanche)</u>

'Kenneth was such a lovely man. He was always fun and so professional. I used to love watching him because they'd give him a few lines, which probably in terms of film time would take about a minute to do, and then you'd watch him elongate it into about ten minutes! He just knew how to perform comedy and make people laugh. It was absolutely instinctive with him. But not only that, everyone loved him.

'I learned a lot from just watching him and watching what he did with what he was given, in terms of his lines, and how much he could get out of a part. I think you learn from everyone you work with without always realising it. But by the time I'd worked with Kenny, I understood why things worked and how to get so much more out of a character and comedy in general if you played it right.

'He was naturally very funny and a real rascal all the time! I've worked with some really great comedy actors who could be quite dour off camera, but Kenny was never like that. He was always fun, lovely to be with, lovely to chat to and a real family man.

'Kenny used to love his Guinness and my special memories are of sitting with him at The George pub in Swaffham after filming *'Allo 'Allo!*, with his pint reminiscing and chatting about the *Carry On* films, as well as other highlights of his career.

'He should not only be remembered as a great actor, and someone who was magnificent at his craft, but as a truly lovely person. I think that is the mark of a really great performer.'

Guy Siner (Lieutenant Hubert Gruber)

'Among the most frequently asked questions I hear from fans of *'Allo 'Allo!'* is "what was your favourite moment from the show?" One above all stands out in my memory, where Lt. Gruber is ordered to interrogate Monsieur Alphonse about suspicious activity in the area. Poor gentle Hubert is completely at a loss until instructed to use the 'Manual of Interrogation'.

'An actor, especially in comedy, has a sort of 'third eye', a part of his brain which looks in from the outside – hitting floor marks, watching camera cuts, observing audience reactions for timing and so on – and I remember vividly watching Ken, as his character came up with ever more unlikely explanations as to why mounds of earth were suddenly appearing in the local graveyard ("could it perhaps be the moles?"), his face conveying with a tiny glance or movement of an eyebrow, his utter discomfort. He was so subtle, so still, so truthful. A consummate comedian. And I was thinking: I am working with a legend. Wow.'

Bobby Warans (Property Buyer)

'I was a huge fan of the *Carry On* films, so to meet Kenneth was wonderful. I loved working with him and found him so warm and approachable. I remember he was so naughty and very cheeky on *'Allo 'Allo!*, but always the total professional. No-one had an entourage, and there were no hangers on. It was just a case of turn up, know your lines and do it. What a shame it's not the same today!'

Charles Garland (Assistant Floor Manager)

'As Monsieur Alphonse, the undertaker in Nouvion, Kenny was at his comedic best, creating a unique and memorable character as he had done in so many *Carry On* films.

'Part of my job as ASM (assistant floor manager) was to look after props and artistes, and I liked to see Café René looking its best with fresh flowers on each table. At the end of each studio recording (on a Friday evening, allowing the cast and crew the weekend off), I would wrap any unused flowers in our prop room at BBC Elstree, and take them to Kenny's dressing room, so that he could take them home to Micky. It was a small thank you to her for spending yet another evening alone, and allowing us to have the pleasure of her husband's wonderful company once again.'

Roy Gould (Ist Assistant Director)

'In one episode of *'Allo 'Allo!'*, Monsieur Alphonse was serving Madame Edith (Carmen Silvera) a meal in the back room of the café. Kenny was meant to do a bit of business with a pepper mill (the full Italian stuff!). For a joke at the dress rehearsal, I got props to find me the biggest pepper mill they could find – they found one over three feet long, it was huge! I set it at the back of the room and waited. Ken started the scene with Carmen and then turned upstage for the pepper mill. Without so much as a pause, he picked up this damned great mill and played the scene, as the crew fell about laughing. Meanwhile, I tried to keep a straight face. As soon as the scene was finished, he pointed at me and chased me round the studio shouting that he would get me back! Ken loved practical jokes and was such a pro.'

While working on *'Allo 'Allo!*, David Croft and Jimmy Perry's sitcom *Hi-de-Hi!* was also enjoying a long-run on BBC One. When original cast member

Leslie Dwyer died in December 1986, the show was left without its Punch and Judy Man. The replacement entertainer part was offered to Kenny.

Kenny went on to become great friends with *Hi-de-Hi!* cast members Paul Shane, Jeffrey Holland, Sue Pollard and, of course, Felix Bowness. All the filming was done at Warners Holiday Camp in Dovercourt, Essex, and the atmosphere of the place put everyone in a holiday mood. All the team had a great time. Well, all except poor Jeff Holland, whose character was always getting thrown into the swimming pool! A pool that was icy cold – every time! The filming was done out of season, of course. There were plenty of enjoyable parties during the location work and one of the team recounted to me:

'Cor, what a laugh your dad is. He's a bugger when he gets on the red wine, we couldn't get him down off the bar table for laughing so much'.

Robin Carr (Production Manager)

'Kenneth's character was required to play a scene in a bath, possibly with Su Pollard. No, she wasn't it the bath as well – it wasn't that sort of show! Although David always wanted to make an episode called 'What Really Happens At Maplins' for transmission after 11pm (true!).

'We shot the scene on location in Dovercourt. We built a bathroom set in the corner of The Hawaiian Ballroom. A hosepipe was connected to the drain so we could get rid of the water, but there was no water supply. Stage management stood around with buckets of hot or cold water (stage management being me, production manager), Roy Gould (assistant floor manager), another assistant floor manager and a couple of prop guys.

'No matter how hard we tried and how often we added hot water, it remained cold. In a cold barn of a building. Bitterly cold. The crew were all wrapped up in hoodies, body-warmers, anoraks, scarves, gloves, etc. Ken was wearing only a pair of flesh-coloured briefs. He was over seventy-years-old! It was so cold that his teeth were chattering. He couldn't speak – he was so cold. Being Ken, everyone laughed at the chattering at first, thinking this was him being funny; no, it was him being cold. As he was given notes of performance by the director, he couldn't reply – his teeth were chattering so much! But as soon as the director said "Action" the chattering stopped and the acting began. It was the most astonishing transformation from an actor I ever witnessed.

'Ken was one of life's good guys. The sort of bloke that if you died and could decide how you live your life over again, you'd keep him in the story.'

On the fateful date in 1987 when the hurricane hit England, they were filming footage for the last series of *Hi-de-Hi!*. Kenny was due home the next day. Micky was worried and rang me, saying he would be back early morning after staying over at Dovercourt. Telephone lines were down in many places and she had not been able to make contact, so I drove the twenty odd miles from my home in Chesham to keep her company at Home Oaks. When I got there, Micky was looking a bit puzzled.

'He must be on his way,' she said. 'I've just had a phone call from Sue Pollard asking if he was home yet, as he had left his dressing gown in her bedroom.'

When he finally got home, he was very hung-over – but at least safe!

As *'Allo 'Allo!* grew more and more popular, so did the demand for new series. And with each new contract, Kenny was commanding more money and now earning more than he had ever done on TV before. Everything was running smoothly and life was good until January 1990 when Gordon Kaye had a near-fatal accident. During a storm force gale, a scaffold plank flew through his windscreen in London and hit him in the head. The next series was put on hold and everyone held their breath.

Kenny then fell ill and was diagnosed with stomach cancer. He kept this so secret that only his doctor knew, not even Micky. He finally had to tell her when the doctors said they had to operate. Jean Diamond (his agent) was told not to tell the industry and even I never knew it was cancer until recovery was complete and he was given the all clear. Talk about being 'a private person'!

Kenny's cancer had been put down to smoking. He used to smoke while eating and would often have an ashtray by his side at the dining table, thus ingesting the smoke. When he came out of hospital he never smoked again and never mentioned missing the habit. He went back to work with half a stomach, a strict 'No No' diet and carried on as if nothing had happened. He was weakened by the operation and moved around cautiously. To beging with, his temperament was that of a severely reprimanded boy who knew he had done wrong. But he was soon Kenny again and back in the swing of things.

Kenny made a guest appearance as psychiatrist, Professor Heindrich Van Manheim, in an episode of *You Rang, M`Lord?* Then *'Allo 'Allo!* went back into production. A good family Christmas was had at Home Oaks. All three of his grandchildren there, including baby Alice, who was born shortly after Kenny had come out of hospital.

Having just mentioned Alice, this seems like the right moment to include her memories of her late grandad:

'As the youngest grandchild, I have very few memories of my grandad Connor, as he died when I was just three-years-old. The only vivid memory I have is of him walking through the entrance hall of 'Meldrum House', with grandma Micky and our family dog, Buster, being really excited.

I suppose I am both lucky and grateful for grandad's career, as it has meant that not a week goes by when I can't see his cheeky face or hear his funny voice on my TV. I would love to have been able to grow up with him around a little longer. I think my life would be quite different!

'I have always enjoyed listening to my dad's stories about his life as a child, growing up with Kenny as a 'Pops'! It always sounded like the real life *Just William* or the boys' version of *St. Trinian's*!!

'I often get my dad to tell me the same stories over and over again. Like when grandad nicked the roast chicken out of the oven at Home Oaks and fed it to the hungry boarding school boys – including dad – over the playing fields fence. And how he would take dad`s school trunk up to the school at the start of term and dump it outside the teachers' entrance! Dad used to get embarrassed, as all the other kids had theirs brought in by their dads' Rolls Royces.

I would go with Kenny for his six-month check-ups and he was clear of any cancer, but one of the checks revealed a collapsing artery that lay near the spine. It became clear that another operation was needed. It was risky and too near the spine to tackle from the shortest route. They had to open him up and go through from the front, past all of his organs. He was in intensive care for over a week, improving and then slipping back again into delirium, and this brought fear, hate and ranting. One of the nurses was German and he picked up on the accent.

'Piss off, we used to kill you bastards,' he barked at her.

Fortunately, the nurse took it well. When poor Micky heard of this incident she explained that Kenny was in *'Allo 'Allo!* and must have thought he was acting.

Kenny, of course, made it through, but the ordeal knocked the stuffing out of him. His body a mass of scars and he never got his strength back. One of the surgeons said they would not usually perform this sort of operation on a man of his age and the decision to go ahead was because it was Kenneth Connor, a national heritage. It was their duty!

'Thanks,' said Kenny. 'I wish you hadn't bothered!'
They laughed.

By now, I was working with David Croft, along with his long term assistants, Charles Garland and Roy Gould, who showed me the way the boss liked things done. We were working on the third series of *You Rang, M'Lord?* Like me, Charles Garland still looks back on the days with great fondness:

'I was asked by my boss if I would be interested in producing a "proving trial" of the newly-refurbished

163

Studio C at BBC Elstree. New equipment had to be tested to ensure that everything worked perfectly before going into service, and providing broadcast programmes, so a test run was needed. I devised a themed chat show. Entitled, *It Makes Me Laugh*, it featured radio presenter and accomplished interviewer, Simon Cummings (County Sound Radio in Guildford), talking to special guests, Kenneth Connor and Les Dennis. The question posed was "What's the difference between a comedy actor and a comedian?" Kenny, as usual, was wonderful, funny and fascinating, and Les as charming and fun as always.

'I got to know Kenny and Micky well, and, of course, met Jeremy and his beautiful family soon afterwards. Jeremy is like the younger brother I never had, and once he had been recruited into the BBC, became a much respected colleague, and huge fun to be with. Working with Jeremy also meant spending more time at Kenny and Micky's house, which was lovely.

'The Connor family home in Harrow had three prominent gate posts. On the first, the word "HOME" and on the second "OAKS". Kenny told me that he always wanted to complete the third post by adding "EXUAL".

'When my daughter, Jo, reached a significant birthday, Charlie Leatherland, a talented artist and designer, and son of my good friend Vicki, created a wonderful portrait of Jo. Kenny, Micky and Jeremy came to our house for a family party, and Kenny said he'd like to buy a frame for the portrait as a present for Jo. There was no big announcement or flamboyant gesture, just a subtle word in my ear, and it was done. It is now a family heirloom, of course.'

Yes, Charles had a lot of time for Kenny!

When I was working on my first series of *You Rang, M'Lord?* I found myself in a dilemma. Not only was it my first time working for David Croft, it was Kenny's first as a recipient of an honour from the Queen! The timing was not good, though, as I could not go to Buckingham Palace to see him receive his MBE. Unfortunately, the date clashed with the first day of principal photography in my new role and I thought it would be bad form to go, especially as David Croft had given me the position. I asked Charles what I should do, but we could not come up with the right decision. In the end it was dad who came up with the answer.

'The show comes first,' he said. 'Anyway, you can come next year for the Knighthood!'

Some months later, I was at lunch with David Croft.

'You could have gone, you know,' he said.

'Sorry? Gone?' I asked, somewhat confused.

'Yes. Buckingham Palace,' he replied. 'You could have gone.'

During the summer of 1992 we dd some filming for *You Rang, M'Lord?* in Norfolk. As Kenny had been in remission from cancer since the surgery, we decided to invite Kenny up to visit the unit and booked him a room at the unit hotel, The George in Swaffham. I was worried all day while filming, as he had chosen to drive up and after his operations he did not have much stamina. I kept wondering if he would make it. But on arriving back at the hotel at the end of the day, there he was in the bar with Jeff Holland and Paul Shane – and a glass of white wine! Kenny had a great four days with us, visiting the locations for lunch and sitting with Jimmy Perry and David Croft watching the progress, taking the piss out of me and generally joking with the crew.

One afternoon in Swaffham I spotted Bill Pertwee and a few of the actors ambling along in the sun.

'Jeremy,' said Bill. 'Your dad has just treated us to a lovely lunch with beautiful wine at The Grange.'

He was beaming.

'Where is he now then?' I asked.

'Oh, he`s gone back to the hotel for a siesta,' he informed me.

I went to see him in his room later and he said he would lay low that night. 'I`m doing okay though, eh, son?'

The year 1992 marked a first for David Croft too. He had all but taken over the BBC Acton Rehearsal Rooms with three of his productions – *'Allo 'Allo!*, *You Rang, M'Lord?* and *Grace and Favour* – being rehearsed there. 'The Acton Hilton' nickname was replaced with a new one – 'Croft Towers'. The roof top restaurant was now the green room for the large Croft Repertory Company. All of the stars from Croft's sitcoms could be found there, trying to out act each other at the self-service counter. The noise was amazing and other BBC staff started to shy away. We on the production teams had a hard time of it, trying to keep track of our own actors as they were in and out of each other`s rehearsal rooms for a gossip!

One morning, I ran to catch the lift in reception and crammed myself in. The door shut and then there was the usual early morning silence of acknowledgement as we travelled up. Suddenly a little man pushed through all the others and presently punched me right in the stomach.

'You`re late!' he shouted.

I doubled up and dropped my bags.

'No, I`m not, dad!' I said, wincing.

Chapter Eleven

Swiftly And With Style

With *'Allo 'Allo!* and *You Rang M'Lord?* now finished, it was a quiet start for me in 1993. Work ran dry in the May, so we planned a trip. In June, Kenny and I took off for a week in Portsmouth to revisit his home town and his old haunts. We walked the defense walls of Old Portsmouth and stayed at the Sally Port Hotel, opposite the cathedral. We walked a lot and Kenny thought a lot and slept a lot, but ate very little. He told me tales I had heard before and I still loved them. We ate white fish and drank white wine, as it was gentle on his stomach. He started asking me to get a rum and peppermint cordial for him in our room at the hotel when he rested.

'Since when have you been drinking that?' I asked.

'The doctor said I should try it if my stomach played up,' he replied.

We went on board the HMS Warrior, the Victory and visited the Mary Rose. We got on to the water and cruised around the harbor, talking about what work we might expect. I had a call from the BBC at the hotel telling me I was wanted for *The Alexei Sayle Show*. We waved Portsmouth what we hoped would be a temporary fond farewell and headed back to London.

The Alexei Sayle Show, which I began working on in the July, proved to be a pig of a programme. Kenny was also suffering with with his own pig of a pain. I started visiting Home Oaks a few times a week, just to see how my parents were doing.

Not long afterwards there was a meeting with the doctor and tests were run. The cancer had returned and Kenny had to have chemotherapy. He was upbeat with this and drove himself to the hospital for treatment twice a week. He began to feel better and we started going round for Sunday lunches again. Just Kenny, Micky and me, Terri (my wife) and the kids. He was getting frail with the treatment, but was still on good form.

I went filming again and, on my return, at the beginning of October, Kenny was not well at all. The GP was making regular visits and Micky was very quiet. She asked the doctor to explain the situation to me. The stomach cancer had spread to Kenny's liver and it was not curable. It was just a matter of time. It was thought that he might have a year if he reacted well to the chemo. I took a back seat from Alexei's show and visited home more often.

There was an occasion when Kenny rang me at my home asking for help to take some black sacks of autumn leaves to the dump. I went over to help and he was in the garden with the bags. They were feather light, yet he could not manage to lift one bag into the boot.

I moved on to my next show, *Nelson's Column*, for pre-Christmas location filming in Oxfordshire. I think I'd only been there a couple of weeks when I had to go back. Kenny had just made a guest appearance on *Telly Addicts* and had only just made it. Kenny rang the hospital on Monday 22 November to cancel his chemo, saying he wouldn't need it again. He took to his bed. The doctor increased his morphine and booked Macmillan nurses to visit him. Micky brought him small bowls of food and I moved in to Home Oaks.

By now, Kenny was in a lot of pain, and one day he sat on the edge of the bed rocking himself. He took my hands, looked at me angrily.

'I only wanted five more years,' he said. 'That's not too much to ask, is it?'

On Thursday 25 November, Kenny decided to have dinner downstairs in the breakfast room. It was there that he wanted us to have drinks.

'But dad, what can you drink?' I asked.

'Give me an Advocaat in a Schnapps glass,' he replied.

Charles Garland also has some appropriate memories of this time to add at this juncture:

'Time and work moved on, and Kenny became older, and less well. One Friday afternoon, I answered the telephone in the office. It was Jeremy.

'Dad's asking to see you. Do you think you could call in at some point?' he said.

I made one of the best decisions in my life.

'I'll come over straight from work – see you in an hour,' I replied.

When I arrived, Kenny was sitting in his favourite chair. He looked small and frail, but he greeted me with a smile and a hug. Micky brought me a glass of wine, and we sat and chatted. Jeremy was quiet, and let his dad chat with me. After a while, Micky came over to Kenny. All those years in Harrow and her Geordie accent was still firmly in place.

'Is there anything I can get you, pet?' she asked.

'Kiss please,' was his reply.

Micky leant over and gave him a kiss. Kenny turned to me, winked and gave that impish grin I had seen so often. Eventually it was time to leave, and I drove home to Godalming re-living the evening in my mind.'

I got a simple meal ready with Micky and went to get Kenny. When he walked through the door he sat at the table. The meal consisted of Birds Eye cod in parsley sauce with mash and peas. Kenny had his Advocaat, Micky a whisky and I had wine. We talked about the garden and Portsmouth and then he returned to bed and we tucked him in. Micky went to check on him a bit later and called out for me. He had fallen out of bed and I struggled to lift him back in. I wondered how he could be so heavy, given there was nothing left of him. The nurses and our GP came and we stood around him. The doctor giving him a shot of morphine.

It was late evening on Saturday 27 November when Kenny let out a big sigh.

'He`s gone,' I said.

One of the nurses took my arm and took me away from the bed.

'Sometimes they can still hear you,' she whispered in a soft Irish voice.

One week ago he had made his final appearance, and now he had left the stage door into the night for the last time, his cap pulled down over his eyes.

After the doctor had paid his visit, and the funeral directors had carried Kenny away, the nurses gave words of comfort, a grieving call card and then, hugging us, they left.

Micky and I sat at the table in the morning room drinking tea laced with whisky. I was numb. Micky was rocking herself back and forth on the chair she sat in, her eyes as wide as saucers and vacant. With a hand on the table that held a cigarette of un-flicked ash, curling smoke away over her painted nails.

'What are we going to do now?' she kept asking.

We sat like this until the dawn brought cold winter light and the gas boiler behind me fired into life, bringing warmth to the dormant radiators that now started to creak. We had been sitting through the night unaware of the freezing cold.

'Why don't you go and make some fresh tea and maybe some toast and marmite. We need to eat,' I suggested. 'I'll lay up a new fire in the sitting room. Make it a real roarer.'

The fire was slow to catch and Mate's voice came to mind saying 'Brasso'. So I poured a little Brasso on to an old duster and poked it into the centre and 'Woosh!' it burst into life. We carried tea and toast to the sitting room and sat looking at the fire. The newspaper flopped through the letterbox on to the floor, making us jump. There's still life out there. After holding its breath, Home Oaks had started breathing again. Warmth was returning, and hot water was pumping through its veins.

I went into the hall and rang Jean Diamond, who was Kenny's agent, and told her that he had died in the early hours of the morning. It felt uneasy saying these words, like ill-fitting lines in a script. She agreed to contact the press, the BBC and producers. I stayed by the phone taking in what I had just said. It was out there. I'd said it. Kenny was dead. This wasn't the first call I had made. As soon as the nurses had left I'd rung my wife, being the most immediate of family. Terri was shocked that it had happened so suddenly and extremely upset that the grandchildren had not been by his side. I still don't think this would have been a good thing, or a healthy idea. I think the kids regarded him then, as they still do now, as a mad grandad in a whacky house. Not the crumbled, defeated hero who had left in pain and feeling cheated. This he had shared with me, and me alone. To all around him, he had slipped away with dignity and done so privately.

Charles Garland learned a valuable lesson, which he wanted to share in this book:

'If I had waited twenty-four hours, I would never have seen him again. This was a huge lesson to learn

171

– never put off visiting someone who is sick or asking to see you.'

JOKE TIME!! Bob Monkhouse was a great pal of Kenny's, so here's a fitting one from him:

'When I die I want to go like my dad, peacefully and in my sleep, with a smile on my face. I don't want to go frightened and screaming, with anguish on my face like his bus passengers.'

I picked up the phone again and started ringing family and friends. Then Micky spoke to her relatives in Northumberland. The problem was as soon as we put the phone down, it would ring again with someone who had just heard the news. The phone rang constantly all day and into the night as the news spread around the world. This was an overwhelming statement to the love and respect that was felt for Kenny. People were ringing with their sincere condolences. People rang in tears. They rung in disbelieving sobs. They rang to share their despairing grief, while others spoke of the fun times they had had with Kenny. It was exhausting. I felt like I was running a bloody counselling call line! I went to get the milk between calls and there on the door step was the fresh milk, together with an empty bottle with a message of condolence from the milkman.

The funeral director knocked at the door and apologised for calling unannounced. He told us that he could not get through on the phone and needed to sort the arrangements. By coincidence – as I had not contacted them but the doctor had – it was the same family company that had undertaken Mate's funeral. That felt good. He asked which church we had booked. Micky and I quickly decided on St Mary's, Harrow-on-the-Hill, and I rang and spoke to the vicar, who said he'd be delighted to host the ceremony. I put the phone down and it rang again. That`s when we decided to take it off the hook. We needed a break for half-an-hour. And so the day continued this way until night fell and Micky and I decided that the phone finally had to come off the hook before the six o`clock news started. We watched it while eating boiled eggs with soldiers and wine.

At about eight o`clock the doorbell rang. We looked at each other with pained faces.

'Oh God, who could that be?' I said.

I went to the door.

'Who is it?' I asked.

'It`s me,' a small voice replied.

I looked through the spy glass and saw Annie looking up into the lens. She was clutching something. Where had she sprung from? I hadn`t seen her for years. I opened the door.

'I saw the six o`clock news,' she told me. 'I tried ringing, but I couldn`t get through. I`ve brought you some soup.'

She held out a large thermos flask.

'Who is it?' Micky shouted in a firm voice.

'It`s Annie,' I replied.

'Well, don`t leave her out there, man!' she exclaimed. 'Let her in!' .

I took Annie into the sitting room and Micky stood up and hugged Annie.

'I'm so glad you've come' she said warmly.

Annie was my first girlfriend and used to spend hours at Home Oaks cooking with Micky. This happened in our teens.

Annie stayed a couple of hours and heated up the soup for us. She gave out advice on how to deal with our new grief by telling us how she had dealt with the death of her dad, Colin. He had died six years earlier, also of cancer, at the young age of just fifty-seven. She was a great help to us and she left promising to come to the funeral.

We then decided to call it a day and turned the lights out on an awkward and strange experience.

The next few days leading up to the funeral were occupied with the usual post death paraphernalia of organising the service, changing bank details and, of course, the reading of the will. I drove Micky to a solicitor's office in Watford and found it up a shabby side street, opposite a pool hall bar. We were half-an-hour early, so we went for a steadying drink in the bar and looked out at the gloomy office we were about to enter.

'By, you do take me to the best of places, Jeremy,' said Micky.

'Fancy a game of pool?' I joked.

'That's surely not our solicitor's office?' Micky asked.

'Afraid it is,' I replied.

'Typical of your father to have some dodgy looking solicitor's place,' she said matter of factly. 'I pity you, Jeremy. His financial affairs are bound to be in a hell of a mess.'

This news did not do anything to improve my solemn mood.

'He was never any good at it,' she continued. 'He just bunged all his receipts in a big envelope and threw them at the accountant. God knows what we'll find. You'll have to sort it, I can't.'

'Drink your whisky,' I pleaded gently.

Micky and I walked across to the office and walked through the flimsy front door, up some rickety stairs and into the box room that was reception. We were told that the solicitor was still at lunch and would not be long. The receptionist then took us both back downstairs to wait in the meeting room that had obviously been the front room of this once tiny residential terrace house. We waited an hour in this characterless room before the solicitor finally arrived. Eventually, we had heard the front door bang open and laughing chatter between two men as they made their way up the stairs. Then, after some creaking about and murmuring, feet finally rushed down the stairs and the solicitor burst into the room with a large file clasped under one arm, while hastily trying to do up his black tie.

'Good afternoon,' he said, like some kind of a joyous publican.

The solicitor plonked himself down in a chair opposite us. He slapped the file down on the table, while tightening the symbol of sympathy around his neck, and smoothing his hair.

'There's nothing to be said really. The entire estate goes to Margaret Irene Connor – who is you, I take it?' he said, smiling at Micky. 'Oh, and five grand to his sister, Iris! There's some pretty useless shares and some premium bonds that don't count for much. I'll sort the probate paperwork and that's the job done really.'

We left the office and walked to the car with a feeling of acceptance about this meeting. It was typical of Kenny's actions when it was anything to do with sensibly organised legal or business matters.

'I want something to eat,' said Micky. 'And don't take me to another dive bar. I want to go to a decent pub.'

On the morning of the funeral, the caterers arrived at nine o'clock and dropped off the finger buffet. Bobby

Warans had organised this for me. Bobby is the master of the art of set dressing and prop buying and his 'can do' is actually 'done luv'. He used the same caterers for production hospitality requirements and they weren't the usual, and certainly not your carefully arranged, BBC triangles of gala pie and cheese on a stick! Try instead, black and red caviar on rye bread, presented as a chess board. Oh yes!

Unfortunately, there was no champagne. No wines. There was no bar to set up. Micky had flatly refused to have that as an option. Everything for 'a nice cup of tea' was already in place, and all there was left to do was wait. A short while later the vicar rang.

'Hello Jeremy, how is your mother bearing up?' he asked. 'The church is all prepared and waiting,' he said soothingly. 'The Order of Service sheets have been put out and it's not raining.'

Then he could not contain himself any longer.

'Now, I know you said no press or TV to be anywhere near the church, but I had a phone call from a lovely lady at an ITV newsroom,' he informed me. 'They said they really needed to be here. And they are! They're here!'

My worst nightmare was coming true.

'I have told them not to come inside the church grounds,' the vicar enthused. 'And they say they can shoot what they need from the roadside. They want some background coverage of the hearse with the coffin and the various floral tributes! She said something about just enough to do a piece to camera. Well, you probably know what that means.'

I grunted and put the phone down. This really pissed me off, as it was not what my father would have wanted at all. 'They can shoot', 'Coverage', 'Piece to camera' – the poor old vicar's using their lingo now. He's been got at and loving it. I was thinking all these bad things of the poor vicar when Terri and the kids turned up.

Everyone was very ill at ease and we decided on a stirrup cup. Having our very young children around us lifted our spirits anyway. The rest of the day remains a sort of a oneness to me, but these vivid memories remain.

The hearse and following cars arrived at the same time as the refuse truck. Yes, Kenny was being disposed of on the same day as the rubbish! I remember thinking that I wished he was here to see this. I wanted to recheck the will to see if he had requested it to be there! I could see him jumping up out of his coffin and addressing the funeral director.

'Do you mind, I`m not paying hard earned money for your over-priced services. I`m a rate payer, you know!'

And then him turning to the dustman to deliver his final ever punch line.

'Oi, wait for me lads! I`ll jump up on the cart!'

As the cortege drove off down the road, the refuse men doffed their caps off and stood still while we passed. I looked at them and found myself humming 'My Old Man`s A Dustman', while grinning and waving at them. The toll gate was open and the gate keeper was standing upright and stock still.

When we reached the bottom of South Hill Avenue, we turned on to the Northolt Road, tagging behind a double decker bus! We arrived at Saint Mary`s five minutes later to see the small news crew standing around. They didn`t look at us, let alone point a camera as we walked up the path into the church. It was packed and we were amazed by this. Hymns were sung and prayers were said. I looked around at the audience. David Croft was there with Roy Gould and Charles

Garland, and my senior production manager at the BBC, John Adams. Kenny's agent, Jean, was also in attendance along with many other showbiz contacts. Annie, Michael Popper, Terri and our kids, plus lots of her family, were all seated present too. Finally, a cousin, Sam, and his wife, Margaret, had travelled down for the funeral from Northumberland.

Charles Garland gave a fantastic eulogy that really gave polish to the funeral.

Charles was keen to share how he felt about his contribution to the day:

'I was surprised and deeply honoured to be asked by Jeremy to speak at Kenny's funeral. I tried my best to pay tribute to one of the most quietly generous, modest, but totally hilarious men I have ever had the pleasure of knowing.'

The next thing I remember was getting back in the car for the journey to Ruislip Crematorium. As we walked back down the path, I saw the camera pointing at us and following us. I used an old trick that had been passed on to me. I stared straight 'down the barrel' of the camera with my best foul, murderous look – a bit like opposing football hooligan 'fans' do before they kick in their heads.

Annie Connor – who later became my wife – recalls the following about the day of Kenny's funeral:

'When the service was over, I was passing the car taking Micky and Jeremy to the crematorium. Micky stopped me and asked me to go to the crematorium. I said that it was private and family only, so I shouldn't. She said that I counted as family, as I went way back and Kenny liked me a lot. It was a

178

hard ask. I didn't even go to my own father's cremation, only the church, which happened to be St. Mary's. I couldn't get out of it, so I followed in my car and then on to Home Oaks. I felt out of my comfort zone there too. All these showbiz types were there and it was a bit daunting, even though I'd known Kenny since I was ten and had met some of the *Carry On* stars at times. I hung out with Jem's cousin, Sam and Popper.'

After the service at the crematorium, we went back to the house where those who had not had the pleasure of the service were sitting around talking quietly, cups of tea in their hands. It was a sombre crowd. Terri was already there offering trays of food around. She had decided that the kids should not go to the crematorium, as they were too young. I remember shaking a few hands and a couple of Kenny's friends seemed understandably confused. 'A dry wake then? Not like Kenny!'

I went into the bar and broke out the stock of whisky and Micky's brandies and sherry, and tried to lighten up the atmosphere with filming anecdotes. This worked, triggering off 'No, this is what really happened' type-of-conversations.

By the time everyone had left, I felt happier that a warm send-off had been achieved. Poor Micky had just wanted it to be all over before it began. We watched the news that night and all we saw were the shots of the hearse and I remember seeing a wreath from Joan Sims.

I stayed one more week with Micky until she felt settled enough to carry on and then re-joined my production team. They were filming in and around Oxford for *Nelson's Column*. I set off from my Chesham home one evening in the cold and fog with an empty feeling, wondering how I would be received. Leaving a production in mid-flow for family reasons was very taboo. I walked into the bar of the unit hotel and they were all there. It was a week before Christmas and the bar was decorated and full of Christmas cheer. The producer/director, Susie Belbin, saw me and welcomed me with open arms.

'Give this boy a brandy,' she said. 'Jeremy, I'm so sorry. I didn't realise he was so ill.'

Like Kenny used to say, the show must go on.

Kenny's ashes remained on his bar at Home Oaks until I decided where to scatter them. Then one day, I rang Bob Reader at the marina and said I wanted to scatter the ashes in the river at Bourne End, because it was his favourite spot on the Thames.

Two days later, on a cold winter's morning, I met Bob at the boatyard with Peter Camden, the yard manager, who had the tug running. We jumped on-board and backed out into the fast flowing current and headed up stream. Bob said he did not want to put the ashes over the side in front of the marina, as he was not sure it was entirely legal. We stopped at Spade Oak reach and I slipped the ashes into the muddy waters and watched them being swiftly dragged away by the flood current.

'Right,' Bob said very purposely. 'Back to the marina.'

Pete turned the tug around and gave it full throttle. The old steel vessel flew through the water with the aid of the fast current, the river banks and houses whizzing by like a train window.

Once the boat was moored, I was ordered to follow them to the club house. Bob fumbled through the large bunch of yard keys and opened the club door and walked straight behind the bar.

'Okay,' he said. 'What's your poison?'

We stood at the bar talking and toasted each other for our successful mission.

'Over to the window!' said Bob.

We moved over to the bay window and looked out over the river.

'Right, salute!' he demanded. 'He should be going past just about now!' he remarked.

'Eh?' I said dumbly.

'Kenny's doing his sail by right now,' he replied.

I laughed and imagined his ashes swirling by in the dark waters. We stood in silence saluting the actor and the founding director of Bourne End Marina.

Micky died six years after Kenny from heart failure – a broken heart. I sold Home Oaks shortly after to a lovely Lancashire lass, the Sky News TV anchor and reporter, Kay Burley. She only had to move across, the road from her house. There was an interview printed in a newspaper about Kay living in the house. During the interview, she claimed that she had been haunted by the late Kenneth Connor. She mentioned that papers would suddenly fly around her office. Well, Kay, if you read this, you are not being haunted by Kenneth Connor – it's Micky Connor! I buried her ashes under her favourite tree. The blue tree, she called it, a Ceanothus, which you built an extension over. Oh yeah, the Geordie blood would be boiling!

Physical evidence that Kenneth Connor existed can be found at Pinewood Studios, where there is a blue plaque erected in his memory. It can also be found in the courtyard at the Globe Theatre on the South Bank in London, where there is a paving stone with his name inscribed on it. It was by a pizza outlet the last time I looked! Well, he did like his Italian food! This flagstone is there due to Micky. After her husband's death she could never go to bed without the LBC late night chat show on. She repeatedly heard an advert promoting fundraising for the Globe Theatre. If you donated three hundred and fifty pounds, you received a flagstone with the inscription of your choice. And, as there was no gravestone or plaque commemorating Kenneth Connor MBE, she thought this a befitting honour. Micky had been at his side when he went to Buckingham Palace to collect his MBE, so what better place to put a commemorative stone than at a theatre of historical significance.

What remains now are not fading memories, but new generations growing up and discovering Kenneth Connor. Thanks to TV, DVD and the internet, children are discovering Kenny's work in the *Carry On* films and the sitcoms, *'Allo 'Allo!* and *Hi-de-Hi!* His new generation of fans often speak to me. The conversation usually goes along the lines of:

'I watched your dad last night. He must be getting pretty old. Is he still working?'

'Oh yeah,' I say with a knowing smile. 'He never stops.'

You have been reading...

Kenneth Connor`s stories` told through his son`s memories.

Any embellishments are a 'Connor trait' and no responsibility can be taken for blatant exploitation of comedic situations. X

Epilogue

Carry On Regardless

After much debate whether to use this epilogue in the book, we decided to include it. Paul was concerned that it was something the fans would not want to be party to, and at the time I agreed wholeheartedly. However, during the course of writing this book many people in the world will have suffered, or be suffering with depression – even lost their lives to it.

When Robin Williams died, I was shocked. I had no idea he was a sufferer. I watched the media reporting the sadness that was felt by so many and, for a week or two, depression was being discussed in the open forum. I was happy that his silent suffering was brought to the forefront, but annoyed that those without media recognition go unnoticed, ignored by the reality that depression is all around us – and, maybe, nearer than we realise.

Here is a contribution about my father in the hope that it goes a little way to promote awareness.

Out Of Work

The come down, the cold turkey of the end of the production is a shock to the system. Your routine of life and work has suddenly gone. For Kenny it was always like a sudden withdrawal of the drug he needed. The realisation there would be no adrenaline rush that night. He felt at a loss, hanging in limbo. But at least he had the garden to return to.

My phone rang at ten am and I answered it.

'It's Sunday, fart face,' said Kenny. 'Coming round for lunch? Roast beef and Yorkshire puddings.'

'Is the pope a Catholic?' I replied cheerily.

'Come over at about ten,' he ordered. 'I need to dig some spuds and the ground is as hard as hell.'

I woke my girlfriend and we went and heaved spuds into the large vegetable pot. We had a great English roast lunch, thus allowing Micky to get back into her routine! Wine was shared, feelings of reunification proclaimed. And as the dusk came on at four thirty pm on a February evening, flashbacks went through our minds as to what scenes we would be doing right now, at that time of the day.

Monday morning. The first day of unemployment. Kenny stayed in bed most of the day.

'Is he up yet?' I asked Micky on the phone.

'No,' she replied. 'It's the usual. He can't get back to the normal life, I just give up. I don't know where I stand.'

Micky had just spent the last three months dragging her shopping trolley back from the supermarket and all she wanted was her husband to drive her there. She never learned to drive. This was due to experiencing a challenging accident in her youth on a bicycle. Micky was so excited to find she was riding unaided on two wheels that she forgot that the brakes were required to stop, and instead aimed the bike at some bushes. They were rose bushes and they tore at her. Micky relied on being transported everywhere after that. I did try and get her to ride one of my bikes. Once she straddled the bike, I tried to explain how to ride it.

'Now, those two levers in front of the handlebars are the brakes,' I said patiently. 'Pull on them to stop. Go on, practice that.'

Micky let go of the handlebars and held onto the brake levers, trying to pull them back – then she fell off, having not moved an inch! There she lay on the driveway in hysterics. Her Geordie accent always came to the front in a hiatus.

'By Jem, yer a bugger, divn't put me on a bike agin!'

Kenny tried to teach Micky to drive. We lived in a private gated road and he felt it was quite safe to teach her there. Out came the maroon Daimler 250 V8 and in went Kenny, with Micky beside her.

'Right Micky, put it into 'D' for drive and just amble forward' Kenny instructed. 'No need to bother about the pedals now.'

Off Micky went, the V8 gurgling at low revs, and up onto the grass verge she went. No matter how many times she tried, Micky always pulled to the left and the safety of the footpath.

Micky walked everywhere, unless her husband was around. He was her lifeline in many ways and he was not aiding her now, in any way. Not when he was immobilised with depression. He needed the help and you always lean on the one you love. When I was a child, and Mate was living across the road, Kenny had family to work on, to entertain and help. His sister, Iris, moved into Stepping Stones to live with her father. She had a troubled life, with many a relationship ending unhappily, and Kenny was there to lend an ear and support her. Iris then moved away after finding a gentle husband who could understand her and she settled in Somerset, withdrawing from the Connor family circle for decades. Now, Kenny's side of the family had moved on leaving a void.

Many press publications say that Kenny was 'A keen gardener'. Was he? To be honest, he certainly wasn't a keen horticulturist, but he needed the garden.

When he was learning a new script or whizzing into Soho to do a voice-over he was animated. He had a purpose. But, when he was just at home he felt rejected, alone in the world even with his family and friends around him. He felt hurt and denied of his justified drug. Money in the bank, but nowhere to go until there was sight of a new job. Gardening may just have been, that 'something to do' in an attempt to keep his mind off his dark thoughts. That's when depression would set in. He'd sit watching TV, damning every show, every actor on their performance. Micky enjoyed her viewing and was used to watching in solitude, with Kenny either being on tour, working at night in the theatre or in bed early when he had to be in make-up for six thirty the next morning. When Kenny was in this damning frame of mind, and it looked as though it was set in, Micky would take herself off to visit her sisters back in Northumberland. He would drive her to Kings Cross and wave her goodbye. Then you would not hear from him while she was away. I would ring him and get no reply. Kenny was always first to the phone, so therefore I always knew something was up. When I did get hold of him, he would make excuses for not being in contact. If I suggested we go for a pub lunch, or took the boat out, he would just say he 'didn`t feel like it' and was 'not in the mood for it'.

Kenny did try to evade his depression with self-help plans. For example, he tried penning poetry, but gave up believing he couldn`t write. Secondly, there were his attempts at 'going for long walks', but that gave him extra time to think about his predicament!! Sod it!!

However, doing physical, brain occupying work helped concentrate Kenny's mind. Once, I went into the kitchen, after I woke up early, to find him at the kitchen sink, wearing only his boxer shorts. He was scrubbing his face, arms and chest with a nail brush. When I asked what he was doing, Kenny said he hadn`t been able to sleep and had decided to saw up logs from the large wood pile we had. He`d been out in the cold of night, striped to the waist, sawing till he 'burnt through the pain barrier'. Kenny then made a mug of tea and went to bed, sleeping till one o`clock. Apparently he did this on a regular basis.

Another therapy was to have a big garden clear up and wheel-barrow the debris out to the gravel frontage of the property and set fire to it. For added 'feel good" factor, Kenny made sure the fires made a huge amount of smoke, dense clouds of it! This, of course, gave unwanted traffic a hazard to negotiate, and he would stand with his rake looking on with distain. Not all these distractions worked.

After one particularly long episode of no contact, I drove the twenty miles from my home in Bucks to Home Oaks. The house was in darkness, curtains not drawn closed. It had a stark, silent, forbidding, *Hammer House of Horrors* feel about it as I pulled up the driveway. I rang the doorbell, tapped the knocker and then let myself in. It was so cold, so damp. My mind was running away with the worst possible scenarios. I called out, but there was no reply. As I walked through the house and into the kitchen, I noticed that all was clean and tidy. No signs of cooking. I went upstairs and into Kenny's bedroom. It had an entrance hallway to negotiate, before the main body of the room was revealed. The large bedroom was being dimly lit by the street lamp. He was laying stock still in his bed staring up at the ceiling unmoving.

'Dad, are you alright?' I asked him. 'What's happening?'

I stood there looking at him, no recognition, no reaction, not even an eye flicker. When I touched his forehead, it was cold and clammy. He finally broke his silence.

'I'm fine,' Kenny said slowly, before starring into space again.

'I've been trying to get hold of you,' I told him. 'What's wrong? Why are you in bed so early? It's not even dinner time. Are you ill?'

His constant gaze did not shift. Kenny spoke again.

'I'm okay,' he told me. 'Go home to your wife and children.'

'But what's wrong?' I replied. 'I don't understand."

'Go home to the warmth of a family,' he demanded.

'I'm family,' I said in a shocked tone of voice. 'What are you talking about?'

Kenny remained silent. He was breathing slowly but rhythmically, his eyes were dead. I did not know how to drag him out of it.

'Look, I'll ring you tomorrow to see how you are,' I informed him. 'No, you ring me. If you don`t, I`ll be over again! That will get you out of bed.'

'Sure,' he said.

I went downstairs and into the bar by the breakfast room. I decided to have a quick drink to help me pull myself together, as I was shocked at seeing him this bad. But here was not a drop left in any of the bottles.

Kenny rang me the next day, nice and early, full of the joys of spring. We never mentioned this episode to each other, but we were so close that we did not have to.

****

Family counts. Friends count. But mainly, those you can trust with anything you might say, count. Those who have no side, nor words of wisdom. Those who are able to look, listen and coax. And there are many of those, more than you may think.

Hey! The Green Cross Code Man's words apply here if you need to help: Stop, Look, Listen and Think! Just don't dress up like Darth Vader.